Keeping Mum

Also by Brian Thompson

A Monkey Among Crocodiles
Imperial Vanities
The Nightmare of a Victorian Bestseller
Devastating Eden

Keeping Mum

A WARTIME CHILDHOOD

Brian Thompson

ATLANTIC BOOKS
LONDON

First published in Great Britain in 2006 by Atlantic Books,
an imprint of Grove Atlantic Ltd.

Copyright © Brian Thompson 2006

The moral right of Brian Thompson to be identified as
the author of this work has been asserted in accordance with
the Copyright, Designs and Patents Act of 1988.

Every effort has been made to contact copyright
holders. The publishers will be pleased to make good any
omissions or rectify any mistakes brought to their attention
at the earliest opportunity.

1 3 5 7 9 8 6 4 2

A CIP catalogue record for this book is available from
the British Library.

1 84354 497 0

Designed and typeset by Patty Rennie Production, Portsoy
Printed in Great Britain by
Creative Print & Design (Wales) Ltd, Ebbw Vale

Atlantic Books
An imprint of Grove Atlantic Ltd
Ormond House
26–27 Boswell Street
London WC1N 3JZ

For Clare

Keeping Mum

Chapter One

I AM ON MY STOMACH, HALF ACROSS MY MOTHER'S body. Her skin smells of sleep and – by association – milk. Downstairs, the front door slams. My mother pushes me away and rolls on to her side. Her hair fans out on the pillow and though she is facing the light that streams through uncurtained windows, her eyes are closed. There are tears in her lashes. She is not sleeping but crying. After a few moments, I clamber out of bed.

Maybe I was three, maybe younger. If three, it was the year Hitler assumed the office of war minister and Neville Chamberlain went to see him at Berchtesgaden. A fortnight later, at the end of September 1938, Chamberlain and the French chief minister Edouard Daladier were summoned to Munich to sign an infamous agreement with the Führer and Mussolini. Though I had no way of knowing it, things might have been worse. I might have been born Czech, or even more calamitously as it proved in the end, German. As it was, the sunlight that streamed into the bedroom illuminated a complacent, apolitical family home. Not a happy home, not in the slightest bit happy; but then, what people did with themselves was their own business. This widely shared belief was what gave these bricks and mortar their Englishness.

My father went to work early in order to impress the bosses – but that was just his way. The rest of the road tramped off half an hour later to clerks' desks or jobs in shops, to college kitchens or inspection pits in oily garages. Their wives set about the washing or cleaning; at the end of the morning they stood on chairs to gossip across the garden fences. My mother did little of any of these things but that too was just her way. For her, the world was huge and for the most part shapeless. We had gone up in it by coming to live here, but only in the way a bubble rises from the marsh. Some would say she did not know how lucky she was. The rented house we lived in was modern and the road lined with gener-ous grass verges. Every so often a tree had been planted along the way to add grace and scale and as it happened there was one outside our house, showering blossom in spring. It made no difference to my mother. Those early-morning tears came from something much more deep and dark and incoherent than disappointment with her surroundings.

The back garden of the house was bounded on three sides by high cedarwood fences and had for its lid a milky-blue sky, vaster than anything we could have imagined possible in London. There, in the Victorian canyons of my parents' childhood, the sky was like a piece of fabric cut up in narrow strips and stuffed to fill a crack or stop a draught. In the crowded streets no gutter was without its stalking, strutting pigeons. Rats whose ancestors had seen the Romans plopped down the drains or scratted in the ceiling. The flinty yellow brick of houses and tenements was black with soot and even a little sunshine revealed how dense the air was with dust and grit. Victorian – Dickensian – factories and workshops stood alongside dwellings: yards away from my father's birthplace was a marble-cutting business worked in the open air, the steam-driven saws sending up fogs of fine white powder. My mother had grown up next door to rag-pickers.

Now, in place of all that, a yawning sky, blustery keen air and rain so fresh that it seemed to improve the washing on the line. While my mother's best scorn was reserved for the people she had left behind, her vandalism soon found its full outlet under such an all-seeing eye. She would walk across the chalky borders of the garden and stamp down shows of spring daffodils, or dash the dregs of her tea into the rose bushes, scattering petals. On hot days she would sit on a chair outside the kitchen door, her legs exposed to the crotch of her knickers, her back turned resolutely to the pleasures of the lawn, smoking and throwing the dog-ends at the dustbin. Though she was hardly thirty years old, she dressed like someone twenty or even forty years older, a bundle of garish rags and lumpy cardigans. Congenitally hard of hearing, when she was not being badgered by someone else's speech her expression assumed a startling emptiness. She was inside there somewhere, but on her own.

My father made the transition to the country more easily by playing the part of bluff yeoman. He was in fact a telephone linesman, shrewdly aware that he had joined the most meritocratic branch of the civil service, as Post Office Engineering was in those days. Climbing up telephone poles was merely a way of looking round to see how the land lay. He was ruthlessly ambitious and a quick learner. He already had two voices, one more polite than the other. When he bought shoes, they were brogues. His shirts were check and his jackets sporty. He took himself off every Sunday for what he liked to call a walk round the parish. By the standards of the times he lived in, he was exceptionally good-looking, with a straight nose inherited from his mother and a burly no-nonsense figure, honed by childhood boxing. He wore his moustache clipped in the manner of Clark Gable and smoked both cigarettes and a pipe.

The pipe gave him a curiously authoritative air, as of a young British bulldog, a man of dangerous parts. Although we had come no further than fifty miles from London, men in his mould were scattered all over the dying Empire, implacable and incorruptible. He was exactly the sort of stout fellow who would know what to do when the drums fell silent and the house servants slipped away out of the compound. Instead of the unblinking animosity of the jungle, however, he had a crazy wife and a skinny child, a rented house and a hundred feet or so of chalky mud.

Though this was still a very young garden, it sagged in the middle like a ruined sofa. That same soft curve was replicated by a rose trellis that had already begun to bow for lack of support. The laths were whimsically coated in flaky and weathered blue distemper, a colour to be found inside the house on the bathroom walls. How to explain this oddity, except as an example of my father's restless and chippy individualism, his gift for doing whatever the hell he liked with the material world? The man next door, a retired policeman, explained in a slow country voice how there were special creosotes that could be used on such a thing as a trellis. This conversation took place over the boundary fence. My father simply stared his neighbour down with his pale blue eyes.

'Suit yourself,' Mr Blundell muttered unnecessarily, as his head disappeared from view.

For miles round was chalk. Wherever a section had been cut, say to accommodate a road through the soft and rounded hills, stiff grey topsoil perched like breadcrumbs on an altar of grubby white. There were cliffs of the stuff in forgotten woodland spinneys, stained green by gouts of winter rain. Only half a mile away along the same reef on which our house had been built was a cement works which mined chalk from two huge holes in the ground, connected to each other by a subterranean tunnel. The mixing tank, in which an iron sweep rotated day and night, had a blackboard fastened to its crusty wall. It showed the number of days that had passed without an industrial accident.

My father's mind was baffled by it all. His childhood had been spent looking out on to a small flagged yard with a mangle shed and an outside privy, the only view the upper three walkways of a Peabody building. The yard was bounded by a high brick wall topped with the brown glass of broken beer bottles. It helps explain my father's character. Otherness – not all, but most – was the enemy of his childhood and all his life he retained a truculence towards other people that could be truly awesome. In his world, nobody acted from a disinterested motive. All vicars were poofs, all policemen bent as meat-hooks. Even the most prestigious shops would rook you if they could and in humbler transactions it was impera-tive to check change for foreign coin. A kind word disguised a sinister intention and to be asked directions in the street was the obvious prelude to begging. It made him a mean-minded man. He learned how to dissimulate to his office superiors, but at the family hearth his suspicious mind was given full rein. Even at his death, some fifty years into the future, he was still living behind walls topped by broken glass.

All the same, in this new place he had found for himself, he gave the countryside every chance to seduce him. He bought a spindly and cumbersome pushchair and in this he would walk me to Cherry Hinton, then a bucolic village decorated with straw wisps. Horse-drawn drays delivered beer to the ivy-covered pub, the horses with ribbons plaited in their manes. Always interested in how things worked, my father would bid me watch as the barrels rolled off the dray, cushioned by a huge sack of sawdust, before disappearing down a steel-hooped ladder into the cellar. I seem to remember a track or path that led back down to the cement works, where he would stand, smoking, sometimes holding me up to watch the cement being mixed. Nearby, men coated in grey dust from head to toe sat on the steps of a small green cabin, watching my father watching them. They gargled water from black screw-top bottles and spat it out in silver gouts.

The painted trellis in our garden, the geometric borders, formed a sketch of what someone recently coming into the country would consider a lovesome thing – but it was only a sketch, the roughest of drafts. The chalk mocked the Adam in my father. Some of the chunks his spade turned up were as large as house bricks. His one great success was in the front garden, where a hedge of lavender ran away with itself so successfully that in the summer season brown-faced gipsies would plunder it, breaking off the stems with a blackened thumbnail, before being repelled by my mother with lumps of chalk. They left behind a scribbled mark on the gatepost, which was bad luck to receive but even worse luck to wash off. An Irishwoman a few doors down came to inspect the mark and hastily crossed herself.

'Your bleeding relatives, I shouldn't wonder,' my mother jeered.

The houses on the opposite side of the road were of an

older stock. Once, our more established neighbours had been able to stand in their front rooms, which they no doubt called the sitting room, gazing out from their bow windows on to nature. Now, instead of rooks on sentry-go or ponies stirred to a gallop by some trick of the wind, they had us. Next door but one was a gap in the housing row where one day a side road would be built and more houses added, right up to the borders of a commercial apple orchard. At the end of the road, two massive billboards advertised this promise. We ingrates were the forerunners of 'Homes for the Future'.

I always imagine some architect laying down his pencil on the final drawings of this development and finding them good. Another boat sent out into the ocean of opportunity, another chance for the man in the street to rise to the challenge of the street's design. The Homes for the Future depicted on the advertising hoarding showed a family of cyclists pedalling towards the viewer – mother, father and young boy. They were laughing for joy.

It is a rainy spring day in 1940. I am collecting nuggets of slimy chalk when my father comes out of the back door and, pointing to a Tiger Moth wobbling towards Marshall's airfield, in a weeping sky, asks me whether I noticed him earlier, waving to me. I stare at the plane and the mild panic in my expression amuses him.

'You didn't see me?' he persists. 'I could see you plain as anything.'

'What was I doing?'

'Picking your nose, as usual.'

I can locate this fateful little conversation exactly, to the last white snail hanging on a blade of grass. We were three yards from the back wall of the house, in front of savagely pruned roses. My father smoked as certain actors did then, dragging the cigarette from his lips with calculated and manly vigour. I knew so very little about him but I did, tender though I was, sense a mood of danger behind the bantering.

In fact, he was giving me his Clark Gable. My mother (a rather crazed Vivien Leigh) joined us with two flowered tea-cups. There was much more of this suppressed danger in the adult conversation that followed. I utterly failed to register the importance of what was being said and wandered away. This, as I can see now – only too clearly – was a mistake. When I looked up again, they had gone inside. Soon, what had been promised arrived. The shouting began and there was the sound of breaking crockery. Perfectly secure in a reserved occupation, with only his garden to think about, my father had gone out that morning and volunteered for RAF aircrew.

I must have been in the first year at school. I can remember the name of it – Blinco Grove Primary – but very little else. It seems to me I was only there for a day, during which we played some outdoor game-in-a-circle with a scuffed yellow ball and then were put down on cots to sleep for half an hour or so. I can recall the dust-impregnated blankets and the faintly sour smell of the boarded floor but not a single lesson, nor anyone's name. By stretching my memory to the limit, I can vaguely remember being given Canadian chocolate compressed into a brick inches thick. Was that then, or later?

The route home from school lay through a street of villas that had donated their railings to the war effort, leaving behind soft plugs of lead in the low walls. You turned into the main road by a parade dominated by a fish and chip shop and then crunched across a kind of clinker court to a broad pavement. To people I met along the way, I was some lallygagging freak, a thin and pigeon-chested child who had betrayed the promise shown in my only photograph to date, where I sat plumped in a chair, looking sullen and clutching a toy horse.

There was a man halfway along this road home who sometimes passed the time of day. I was peering into his hedge one afternoon when he came out of his front door, his watery eyes lighting at once on what I was looking at.

'It's a bumblebee,' he said.

'I know.'

'Ah, you know that much, do you?'

We studied each other. The bags under the man's eyes were dark blue, a colour heightened by white stubble and flyaway hair. There was food caked to his chin. He nodded, as if in answer to an unspoken question.

'Yes,' he said. 'I'm doolally.'

I told him my name.

'That's no name for a hero. Don't you want to be a hero?'

At which his daughter came out and shepherded him word-lessly back into the house. The door slammed with enough force to make the knocker clack. I did not know whether I wanted to be a hero and crossed the road with tears in my eyes. Blubbing was something to feel guilty about, like phys-ical imperfection or dimwittedness. On her best days there could be no one more inventively ribald than my mother, yet the slightest sign of turmoil in others plunged her at once into black despair. It was always better to dissemble in front of her.

In the front room was a revolving bookcase, the improb-able first prize in a whist tournament at which my father had of course triumphed. It carried *Newne's Encyclopaedia of Gardening* and nothing else. If, when it was spun, the shelf containing the encyclopaedia came to rest facing the door, Vivien Leigh would be in merry mood. If not, there would be trouble. I sat on the rag rug, spinning the shelves and think-ing about the man called Doolally and what he was doing, whether he was having his tea. There was the sudden smell of scent in the hallway and my mother came in with what she called jam doorsteps. She put the plate down beside me and checked her hair in the mirror, humming.

'I'm just going to pop out for an hour,' she said, far too casually.

My father had already gone. Though I hardly knew him, it seems significant to me now that I didn't miss him more. Without him, the house had taken on a different character. There was no more shouting. The radio was tuned to dance music, tea was sweetened with jam and when the last of the coal was used up, my mother slept inside a fake fur coat, the bedclothes heaped up in a pyramid. When she remembered, she would obligingly warm my sheets with hot water inside a Tizer bottle. Like her, I slept in my clothes. As for the garden, it reverted all too quickly to what it had been before we came there, the borders indistinguishable from the lawn, the lawn itself a tiny meadow.

I spent a great deal of time alone in the house, licking the salty grime from the window and looking down the road to watch for my mother's return from wherever she had been. Between five and six the neighbours passed, trudging home from work. By eight, the pavements were deserted. There was very little traffic and no one we knew had a car, or had ever owned one. When it had been dark an hour or so, with nothing but the wind left in the street, I would take myself off to bed. All the interior woodwork in the house was painted chocolate brown and it seemed to soak up the light furnished by low-watt bulbs. For fear of the dark, I would leave the landing light on. Flushing the lavatory also helped, for then I could fall asleep listening to the cistern grumbling and muttering to itself.

Not to be able to sleep brought on an agony of terror. My parents had given me the back bedroom, not much smaller than their own. Beyond the high fences, the branches of the commercial apple orchard chattered. It was from this direction I imagined the Germans would come, appearing out of the trees like smoke. If not Germans, then ghosts. Alone for too long, I could hear much more than the sighing all houses make when the last light is extinguished. Boots scraped along floors and there was music and the distant hum of voices. Sometimes, having put myself to bed, I heard gunshots.

'That's right,' my mother said with her elaborate sarcasm. 'That's exactly what you did hear. We was all shooting each other. The corpses are buried in Lord Muck's garden.'

'Who's Lord Muck?'

'Work it out for yourself.'

Cambridge was simply a town. The colleges had no place on my map, which was centred on Drummer Street bus and coach station. After 1942, the streets were stiff with Yanks, ambling along with wide shoes and cocky linen hats, their hands in their pockets. They looked fitter and cleaner than the miserable bundles of khaki they occasionally encountered.

'It is usual to salute an officer in this country,' I heard an elderly captain complain to three airmen young enough to be his children.

'Damn right,' some waistgunner or bombardier replied without malice, pushing him gently aside as though he were a rose sucker in our garden.

'Bloody Yanks,' the captain yelled after them, voicing the common opinion.

Then, suddenly, I am sixty miles away in another school, no more than three or four dusty rooms beside an elevated suburban railway station, learning copperplate handwriting, doing simple addition and subtraction and (for suspiciously long periods) drawing on ragged sheets of sugar paper with a thick and greasy pencil. The teachers are surely unqualified: what kind of a place is this, with its whispering somnolence, more like a Mexican hotel lounge than a classroom? I cannot see on to the station platform because it is masked by advertising hoardings, though these do not reach completely to the ground and disembodied legs occasionally walk past, pause, or in cold weather, stamp. The arrival of the trains make the nailed-down sash windows of the schoolroom shudder, a friendly and somehow reassuring whisper from the world outside.

My mother and father have disappeared and I am living with Elsie, my mother's sister. I have no more idea of how this happened than a parcel might have of the workings of the Post Office. It is the first of many holes in my memory. Was I sent away in anger, or for my own protection? Cambridge was one of the safer places to live during the war: who thought up the bright idea of posting me to a house behind the Kingston bypass, ten miles from the epicentre of the Blitz?

Here I am at eight years old, walking to school in New Malden and collecting pearly cobwebs from the suburban hedges with a twig doubled over into a hoop. In the basement of the church building that houses the school, a girl pulls down her knickers and holds up her brown gingham dress to show me what she looks like. She looks plump and well-fed, with a little pot belly and round thighs. She draws attention to a birthmark on her haunch in the shape of a Spitfire. We stand in carbolic-smelling gloom staring at each other, flinching from time to time as snatches of conversation from the street outside seem to fall through a tiled shaft and its grating. I realise what this girl expects in return. I unbutton my shorts before pulling them down to my knees. She doubles over in disbelieving laughter before running away.

She has a friend called Phyllis, a skinny carrotty girl who wears fair-isle mittens in winter. Even the dewdrop on the end of her nose is lovable to me as we walk part of the way home together. She has a neighing laugh and an inability to look me straight in the eye. My aunt and Phyllis's mother confer in Timothy White's, staring at us both from time to time with pursed lips. Uncle Dick is given the job of explaining to me how things are. Phyllis's father is Missing in Action.

'Which means he is more than likely a gonner, see? So maybe it's best to leave the poor little mite alone.'

'I haven't done anything.'

'Course not. Never said you had. But, you know, sleeping dogs. Something like that.'

Dick had one leg much shortened and wore a surgical boot to compensate. He worked on the print side of the *Daily Express*. Of all the hundred kind and good-natured things he said, or may have said, these are the only words of his I can remember exactly. He tousled my hair, bid me stop the fleas from biting and clumped downstairs, one leg at a time. The childless couple stood discussing me in the hall. Auntie Elsie listened to Dick's account of what had been said and I sensed her familiar emphatic nod.

'What you don't know can't hurt you,' she muttered.

There was a great deal of what I did not know. My mother never came once to visit. I can remember my father arriving out of the blue one afternoon and taking me to a distant cinema to see an American war film, *Guadalcanal Diary*, which he barracked vociferously. Because he was in uniform, nobody liked to say much and in fact one or two other servicemen joined in. It was not the war they reprehended, but our principal ally's part in it. We came out into a moist autumn night and walked home 'for the exercise'. It took more than an hour, during which time my father gave everyone who scurried past in the blackout a cheerful hullo, as though he had lived in those parts all his life. To my astonishment, when we reached the house in Knightwood Crescent, he kissed me briefly on the cheek and walked away without a word.

'Well, where is he?' my aunt cried, peering down the street, as though he might be hiding behind a privet hedge.

'He's gone home,' I muttered.

She put her arms round me and crushed me for a moment and then pushed me inside.

In that walk home from the cinema was the essence of the man. In time of war, his part was that of the bluff and trustworthy constable of virtue. The uniform helped. Bulked out by an RAF greatcoat and with his shoes ringing on the pavement, he was offering passers-by a reassurance they may even have needed. Secretive by nature ('What you don't know can't hurt you'), he had risen to become a bomber navigator and a bit of a hero to his crew. But all that was, as he would have put it, his business. I did not know until many years later that when he joined the RAF he was sent to South Africa to train for aircrew. When he took me to see *Guadalcanal Diary* that afternoon, he had only just returned. Other fathers may have made an adventure out of such a long and dangerous sea trip. He never mentioned it.

In 1955, I was walking with him in Cheapside when a broken figure of a man gave a cry of recognition and tapped him for a pound, anything he could spare. He pushed the poor devil away with the flat of his hand. It was, he explained, his rear-gunner from the war years.

'Don't you want to talk to him?'

'Why should I want to do that?'

My aunt was not much more demonstrative than my father but there was a constancy in her that was enormously reassuring. She taught me multiplication and long division, always with a faint air of vexation, but I knew this to be from an inability even to imagine innumeracy. As a young woman she had crossed the river from one of the worst slums in Lambeth to work in City shops as a sales assistant. She was the model of the winsome assistant who gives a momentary lift to the customer's heart. Her mental arithmetic was dizzying and she could parcel things exquisitely. Once a month she sent her sister stiffly conventional letters outlining my situation – a cold, a new pair of shoes, failure to learn even the basics of the piano. These were written in a round and regular hand on pale blue notepaper. The letters went unanswered.

Elsie had made the transition to a respectable way of life far more successfully than my mother. In New Malden, everybody wanted to be like everybody else and set themselves the task of keeping up appearances. People nowadays speak about the sort of community this creates as stifling: I found it very comforting. When people came to tea – and they were mainly elderly ladies looking for solace from this neat and comely young woman – the sponge cake was laid out on a fretted silver stand and there were marigolds in a pot on the tea trolley. Conversation avoided anything in the least controversial and there was great nicety in knowing when to leave.

'Well, dear,' a spindly old crone said, pulling on her gloves and nodding in my direction, 'that little fellow is much happier *here*, I am quite sure.'

My father had brothers, my mother sisters. One of these worked as a riveter at Shorts and I went to stay with her for a couple of days. She took me to the works' canteen, amid great ribaldry. She was a thickset woman with hennaed hair and a wide letter-box smile.

'Your mother's a bleeding princess,' she commented, passing me her pint to sip at.

'And you can keep your opinions to yourself,' Elsie snapped when I was returned home.

'It's the war effort,' Auntie Ivy yelled, laughing uproariously. She was wearing black serge trousers and a pink sweater and chain-smoked what she called Woodies. Every knuckle on her hands had weeping scars and her nails were torn ragged to the quick.

'I hope you've been keeping your yap shut,' my aunt said, pointing a bread-knife in Ivy's face. 'And where's his tie? I sent him to you with a tie.'

I hid my face. Ivy had worn the tie with a white shirt and those same serge trousers to walk out with me and a more elderly woman called Dot. While I threw bread to the ducks, she and Dot kissed companionably and lit cigarettes from each other's stubs.

A third and far more acceptable aunt arrived one night with a Canadian naval officer and a recording of the Inkspots' latest. When it came to the line about the green grass being buried under the snow, the Canadian mimed hearty digging, sending us into fits of laughter. Then he and Dick went into the front room to talk about the war and Elsie and her sister retreated to the kitchen for what they called a conflab. My mother's name and Ivy's were several times mentioned.

The school I went to seems in retrospect suspiciously small and woebegone. Why it was housed in church premises was another enigma, for the first time I walked into a church from choice was to attend my wedding. We were not a churchy family. I assume that I was christened but I had no idea of the rites or ceremonies otherwise. (Church, as my mother pointed out in later years, was not for the likes of us. She was, by her own lights, being perfectly serious.)

One of the lessons I remember best was practising copper-plate script. The examples came in a landscape format exercise book with a brown cover. The text – short sentences of useful facts – was printed above a dotted line on which we copied it with a spluttering steel nib. One example began: *Gum arabic is* . . . but whatever it is, I have completely forgotten. It was lulling and not at all unpleasant work that I associated with mists and castles. The illusion of practising some ancient art was reinforced at the centrefold of the book, where the staples were red with rust. So weak were they that a thumbnail could erase what had once been bright metal. I worried about this. The rust, the mouse-grey paper, were signs that we had been specially entrusted to keep a wavering flame alive.

The pleasure of the day was drawing landscapes with a blunt pencil, so dense with marks, so emphatic that I felt I could go and live in these pictures, walk down the winding path to some chocolate-box cottage and sit inside staring at the bombers flying overhead. They bore swastikas on their wings and tailplane. Fat bombs dropped from their bellies. In other parts of the same picture, rooks flew unconcernedly towards cauliflower trees and animals intended to be squirrels sat complacently chewing.

Phyllis drew princesses with heart-shaped bodices and empty expressions, their toes peeping out from long flounced dresses. They had speech bubbles coming from their lips saying things like *Hello!* and *I love you!* Sometimes emaciated-looking horses stood nearby. In the lunch break, which we called the dinner break, we would all go down to the basement lavatories, where Phyllis stood aghast as the more impudent girls egged on the boys to show their willies. The old dears that taught us sat upstairs, munching on chalky sandwiches and gossiping about butchers and greengrocers.

The general mood was comfy. Many afternoons passed when I felt my head rock and my eyes roll round in my skull, asleep at the desk. When this happened, Phyllis would prod me with her pencil and then look away, frowning. She had a prewar geometry set in a black leather case and would sometimes twiddle the compasses, or measure angles she had scribbled with the protractor. It passed the time. We were at war – nobody could be in any doubt about that – but floating in a bubble just a little off the ground.

'Eat that cabbage,' Elsie would order. 'There are sailors who lost their lives so's you don't have to go hungry.'

'It's from Uncle Dick's garden,' I objected.

'In general. I'm saying, in general.'

With Elsie I went to Hampton Court and – maybe it was the invasion summer – to an outdoor variety show at Motspur Park, in which a plump contortionist sank down on to the muddy boards in the splits position. When she rose, the insides of her thighs were decorated with dark smudges. Her silver knickers, the soles of her feet and the palms of her hands were likewise blackened. As she bent and writhed, a man, possibly her father, played a piano accordion accompaniment, looking ashamed and uneasy.

'Well,' Elsie commented grimly, 'she's got guts, I'll give her that.'

'She's clever, isn't she, Auntie?'

'She is if you like that sort of thing.'

One of the peculiarities of my aunt's house was that the Anderson shelter was erected indoors, filling a room that may have been originally designed as a study. In it, there were four bunks, candles, bottles of tap water and a first-aid kit in a pink biscuit tin. It was also where the Bible was kept. Once in a while Dick would open up the shelter to air it. We lived beside no marshalling yards or munitions factories but at night the Thames gleamed silver only a few miles away. Even so, the bombers gave us a miss, all but the most nervous or perhaps the most callous of them. My aunt, whose sense of the appropriate was as finely tuned as any duchess, ignored the loom of light that bespoke raids on London and would never comment on the conduct of the war. We persisted tearfully with sums and piano practice.

'Your mother can play,' she wailed once. 'What's up with you, that you can't?'

'We didn't have a piano.'

'There's a lot you don't know of what you did and didn't

have. You're too dreamy by half. The world's got enough dreamboats,' she added.

Hitler, whom every child could sketch, who lived a long way away and whose every purpose was malign, eventually sent Knightwood Crescent his greetings. Dick had actually seen a V-1 rocket cut out and dive to earth over London and from that time on we slept every night in the shelter. I was put to bed on the top bunk and these two childless people sat fully dressed with their knees touching, silent and reprehending. An ack-ack battery had been posted to a playing field a few hundred yards away and would open up, firing at the exhaust flames of what everyone called flying bombs. One they missed dived over this neat and regular landscape, with its cherry trees and long lines of privet, and landed forty yards away.

'We're goners,' Elsie said in a matter-of-fact voice while the frame of the Anderson shelter still resonated.

'Rubbish,' Dick muttered. 'Open that thermos and let's have a cup of tea.'

'The gas!' she shouted suddenly.

Dick lifted me down from the bunk. We were all dusted white. He smoothed under my eyes with his thumb. Elsie struggled with the door of the shelter. It would not budge.

'Well,' she said, 'a nice thing, I must say.'

The emergency services dug us out towards mid-morning. The house had been cut in half as if by a bread-knife. The kitchen, the back room and the bedrooms above had simply disappeared, leaving a view of the tennis courts and, beyond that, the bypass. A fireman carried me into the front room, which was ankle-deep in rubble. The piano had been lifted off the floor and was pinned to the wall by long swords of glass, its whole weight supported by them.

'Bugger me,' the fireman said admiringly. He reached with his hatchet and touched just one shard and the piano fell forward with an almighty crash. Elsie and Dick stood with their arms round each other, staring out at the unaccustomed view from the foot of the missing stairs. Everything they owned had been carried away by the blast. Clothes and bed-linen decorated the branches of distant trees.

The front door was still intact and the firemen, who had climbed through the ground-floor windows to release us, obligingly kicked away the rubble so that we could open it. Where once had stood the house that belonged to the bed-ridden mother of the Radio Doctor, our sole attachment to the world of the famous, was now a huge hole in the ground. The street was ankle-deep in roof tiles.

'How many others copped it?' Dick asked.

A fireman jerked his chin at me by way of reproof and lit a dazzling white cigarette. He ruffled my hair.

'What you nice people need is a good strong cup of the old rosie. Right down there. It's all free. They're all ready for you.'

Sitting in front of the tea van, his legs tucked under a folding card table, was an ancient civilian in a white tin helmet. In front of him was a pile of useful paper and – a surreal touch – a bottle of ink should his fountain pen run dry. Hardly able to hold up his head under the weight of the tin hat, he stared at us through cruel wire glasses as we staggered up to report to the council the disappearance of half the house.

'Good morning,' he said politely.

Chapter Two

IT WAS OFTEN SAID IN CAMBRIDGE THAT OF THE three bombs dropped on it during the war, two were by the Yanks. Yet out on the road to Newmarket was a graveyard of B-17s, the fuselages piled two high, some of them split apart like gutted fish, some blackened by fire. In the bellies of these great planes, reefs of expended ammunition were glued to the decking by a whitish amalgam, giving the cartridges an appearance much like an undigested and indigestible meal. On some of the fuselages there were brutal hatchet marks round once-enclosed gun positions and sometimes a scrap of leather or some fibres of cloth remained snagged in the traversing rings. Though they were long dead, these airframes still smelled of glycol and explosive powder. The whole scrapyard was a monumental reproach to native Cambridge hatred.

The way in for marauding children was across a boundary ditch and under the security fence. There were broad avenues down which the wreckage had been tractored, intersected by alleys no wider than a man's hips. Presumably all the signs and prohibitions were posted at the main gate on the Cambridge–Newmarket road. It was such a dangerous and forbidden place that no child would dare go there alone. No gang exceeded four or five. The prize was what we mistakenly called perspex, from which to make rings, or anything else portable. I went because a girl not at all in the mould of Phyllis had adopted me as her momentary plaything. I remember her for stick-thin legs and bruises on her arms. On the way home, this feral child spat in my face and ran away. I sat down in the middle of a stubble field, shaking.

The flying bomb that destroyed Elsie's house ended nearly three years of careful fostering and meant that I was back with my mother. Distressing to me now, my kindly aunt had disappeared completely. Dick's mother lived in Peckham and maybe they went to live there for a while. It was a house I remember from my occasional visits as having the deathly stillness of a Victorian Sunday afternoon about it. The parlour was heavy with drapes and overstuffed furniture. On the mantelpiece, a hummingbird sat wired to a small mossy branch. Though he lived under a glass bell, the war had got to him too and his tiny head had fallen forward, heavy with grief. It is one of the cruelties that a fugitive memory inflicts on others that I should be able to recall this unimportant detail and yet not know how my aunt survived the destruction of her home.

Both my parents owed Elsie a huge debt of gratitude. Whatever was hopeful about life beat inside her like a drum.

Had I been her child and not theirs, things would have worked out very differently. Cautious, orderly, with a sweet deference to authority, she would have coaxed me along a different path, out of the dark forest and into the light. Instead, to my great shame, her name – and the contribution she had made to my childhood – was so swiftly abandoned that it was as if she had never been. Only many years after our narrow squeak at the hands of Herr Hitler did I find out that when Dick died she had found a post as housekeeper to a rich man. He used her more lovingly than her own family. They married and Elsie lived on to a very great age.

A great deal had changed in Cambridge. The lavender hedge my father had planted in front of the house now sagged and swayed, the flower stalks sprawling to the pavement. The green paint of the house door was flaked and pitted, in one or two places raised in bubbles begging to be popped. Round the back, as my mother invariably described the forsaken area of prewar garden, the trellis was flat on its face. A dining chair with a rexine seat had been left out on the lawn one summer's night and remained there, bleached and ruined.

It was clear that I had come back at an awkward time. Inside the house was a faintly faecal smell, intermingled from time to time with the powerful aphrodisiac of a cheap store perfume called Blue Moon. One of my first memories of homecoming was holding up my mother's skirt for her while she drew seams down the back of her painted legs with an eyebrow pencil. Comparison with Elsie's sturdy legs, about which anything above the knee was as unknowable as Patagonia, was inevitable. I watched the line grow while holding at arm's length my mother's smouldering Lucky Strike. There were packets and cartons of them flung carelessly into the shelves of the revolving bookcase.

'Yes, well,' my mother said guiltily. 'It hasn't all been sodding roses here. And you can't blame me for getting bombed out. So don't try that one.'

If she was at all pleased to see me, she concealed it well. After the careful order of Knightwood Crescent, I was astonished by her wild improvisations at house management, most of all by the complete absence of time in her affairs. She might appear downstairs stark naked in high mid-morning, looking for cigarettes, or wake me up with a cup of tea at midnight, her fake fur still on, the fibres wet with rain. She would break off conversations suddenly to demand what day of the week it was. It came out that she had tried to work in low-grade clerical jobs while I was away, none of which she had held for more than a few months. No friendships had come from these forays into the outside world and the only people she knew by first name wore American uniform.

She went out most evenings, coming back by cab. Sometimes her arrival home was announced by the unmistakable roar and whine of a jeep. This hardly went unnoticed by the neighbours: children my own age went out of their way to tell me my mother slept with Yanks. She had never made friends in the road – indeed, before the war had barely left the house – and now she was paying the price. Offering the occasional kind word or bringing people in for a cup of tea in the early years would have made all the difference to her reputation now. My mother was ten times more shy than she was wanton. What drove her to haunt the edge of dance floors or crowded hotel lounges, she would have called, innocently, having a good time. She was looking for love. At home, there was none.

Six doors down from us was an Irish family who had more reason than most to blacken her name: the bad feeling that had once searched them out was now deflected on to us. Mrs Noonan ('that scrawny old bag of cack') was the principal gossipmonger. Her elderly husband was an invalid of some kind and sat on a kitchen chair outside the front door with a blanket wrapped round him, rain or shine. Such a thing could never have been contemplated in New Malden. Rose Noonan, who should have been weeping quietly in the house according to rules of behaviour I had recently quit, sat on the doorstep beside him, a man's check cap on her head.

'Ah now, Patrick, there goes the mad creature with nothing better to do than dance the war away. That pitiful thing with her, that's her son,' she would explain.

The other children of my age were strangers to me. I did not know how to react to them and joined in their play always at the edge of things. In summer there was a daily congregating point. In the field opposite our house (where now stands a pub) a building site had been abandoned at the start of the war. Right in the middle was a huge saucer of sand. In it we invented elaborate games in which kilted Highlanders fired from the kneeling position at London buses, or bandsmen from the Brigade of Guards threatened Jerry pillboxes with their trombones. It was here that adult shortcomings were discussed and the gossip of the street retold.

The war had thickened and coarsened feelings more than I had realised. We had the sandpit to absorb us but older boys roamed the brick-strewn field as far as some allotments, where they taunted the gang next door. Put to enough provocation, these neighbours would erupt through the runner beans and cabbages of the allotments, whirling staves torn from chestnut palings. It amused them, once they had put everyone to flight, to stand in a circle and piss away the dioramas we smaller boys had constructed in the sand. We watched from a ditch overhung with blackthorn, our escape route through the gardens of the first house in the interrupted row. Only a few months ago in New Malden I had walked home with Phyllis being taught the names of flowers and shrubs in just such gardens.

The folk who lived on the far side of the road, whose houses were older and better looked after, did their best to keep up appearances, which they managed in the English manner by never being seen. But war had brought out the animal in children. There was a pillbox in the field that abutted the orchard. I doubt it had ever been manned and the floor was two or three inches deep in black and foul-smelling water. One pastime was to stuff a tennis ball through a weapons slit and send howling toddlers inside to wade about in the dark looking for it, their screams bouncing off the concrete walls. The game was called Gestapo.

One afternoon, a serious young USAAF pilot came to the house to pick up my mother and gave me a Philip's World Atlas. I showed him a book my father's crew had sent me as consolation for the brush with death in Knightwood Crescent. It was signed by them in the overly jovial fashion of the day. Ken, the pilot, asked me what plane my father flew. I did not know.

'This guy's South African,' he said, studying the signatures, beneath which were appended their owner's rank. 'See?'

'Dad is English,' I said. 'But he didn't need to sign it because he's my father and everything.'

'Check,' Ken said miserably. He opened the shiny blue atlas and showed me where he lived in America, above the second *n* of Indiana.

'Are you homesick?'

'For Christ's sake, kid,' he said as my mother came into the room, borne on a gale of Blue Moon.

There were clearly two wars in progress, or if you counted the destruction of Elsie's house, three. In my father's, his gift for excluding emotion from the human equation had seen him rise from a mere aircraftsman (second class) to flight lieutenant. Ken flew by day, Bert by night. He told me many years later that he had especially enjoyed despatching nervous SOE agents out into the dark over France, always bang on the pissy little torches the Frogs waved about far below. But in his tour of service he had also met his and Ken's Supreme Commander, shaking hands with Eisenhower shortly before D-Day. At Arnhem, towing gliders, his was the second plane over the target. He flew twenty-eight missions and the only injury he suffered was a broken nose, when he managed to land badly in a leap from the high board of the local swimming bath during parachute training in Blackpool.

My mother's war was far more secretive. She was probably at her happiest in the three or four brief years the Yanks chased after her. She loved dancing, wore clothes with a wild, untutored flair and milked the men she met unmercifully for love and romance. Her sense of her own worth was non-existent.

'Your mother is nuts,' Ken's successor told me. 'You know that, don't you?'

I gave him back the Hershey bar he had just given me.

'What's this, kid?'

'Stick it up your bum,' I said.

My mother took a broad view of this exchange.

'I don't like him either,' she said. 'But you shouldn't have told him to stick it up his bum. You have to remember about these Yanks, they don't like meeting what you and me would call real people.'

'I hate them.'

'Never mind that,' my mother said grimly. 'You watch your tongue. You never heard Auntie Elsie say bum, did you? No. So I'll have the same standards here as what she had. I know where it comes from, don't think I don't. You've been mooching round with those Irish buggers down the street.'

There was something in her war that was more real than my father's slow progress towards making himself an officer and gentleman. For all the mess she made of things, she was by temperament more likely than he to have sensed the huge ache in the skies that overlaid England, or come to that, Europe. Hers was a tragic war, filled with cupboards stuffed with skeletons. One of her boyfriends gave me his baseball bat and a huge meaty softball. He was killed a week or so later.

'Do you want me to hide it?' I asked practically, thinking of my father.

'What a little dodger you've turned into since you've come home.'

She ran her hands down the neck of the bat for a moment or two and then threw it clattering through the kitchen door into the hallway.

'Play with it,' she said. 'What do I care?'

I was nine years old, a slight child with namby-pamby manners and as much emotional reticence as my mother had herself. Elsie had always commended me to neighbours as being as quiet as a mouse. Ma, on her good days, encouraged a more outward-going attitude – silence in others made her anxious. She quarried me endlessly for evidence that, though quiet, I was not unhappy. On washdays, which could be any day of the week at whatever interval, my frayed underpants hung on the washing line next to her camiknickers. I once tried a joke which depended on the sight of them being tangled together in a high wind.

'They're talking to each other.'

'They'd have a few stories to tell,' my mother agreed.

Elsie's place in my affections was taken by my father's parents, who lived in London, specifically in Lambeth Walk, next door to an awesome old woman called Mrs Broom. She sold second-hand clothes from a barrow outside her front door and about this time of my life, when I was approaching ten, advised me sternly that if I never did nothing else to honour the family – though my father had undoubtedly shown the way by becoming an officer – if I never amounted to nothing very much myself, I should at least metticilate. Nobody knew what Mrs Broom was on about and her admonition was received in stony silence.

'I know what I'm saying, Alice,' she insisted, jerking up her whiskery chin. My grandmother turned to me.

'You don't have to if you don't want to,' she huffed. Earlier in the week, Mrs Broom had told me to sod off out of it when I was playing marbles underneath her barrow. My grandmother came out, flour dusting her arms up to her dimpled elbows, and gave her neighbour one up the throat that sent her reeling. The backfiring remark about matriculation had been intended by Mrs Broom as a peace offering.

Number 15 Lambeth Walk was a tall, narrow house. On the ground floor was a tiny shop, where bicycles were repaired and gas mantles sold, as well as torch batteries, locks, chains and other general chandlery. An oil-stained bench served as a counter, with a huge metalwork vice bolted to it. The bar that closed the jaws was big enough to play at submarines, sometimes serving as a periscope, sometimes as a watertight door. Laid out in empty tobacco tins were odd nuts and bolts my grandfather had scavenged from the gutters of Lambeth Bridge Road and patiently unseized by plunging them into baths of oil. The oil was dispensed from a giant can activated by a thumb trigger, the sort used by railwaymen to reach a distant bearing. Bicycle tyres hung on an improvised rack and handlebars tangled in a corner. What little money that came in from this enterprise was kept in a drawer under the bench. Jockie and Queenie Thompson had brought up four sons from the income, one of whom was the flight lieutenant with the Clark Gable moustache.

The shop led to a dark and windowless passage wide enough to have been a room at some stage in the past. Ranged against one wall were shelves bearing dusty accumulator batteries and naphtha cycle lamps with bull's-eye lenses, beneath which was a drift of boxes and cartons. Some were empty but others stuffed with bric-a-brac, including a miniature harp in an ornate frame, to which bits of gold leaf still adhered. How this had come into the house was a mystery, for no one in that family could play so much as a mouth organ. More explicable was a bugle motor horn with an enormous bulb, or the biscuit tin crammed with clockwork motors. A swarm of door keys hung from a piece of rotting twine and in a cigar box were the ancient tin tokens from the picture house round the corner.

The parlour, where most of the living was done, was dominated by an oven range that Queenie encouraged me to polish with stove blacking. It was a job I loved to do. While I buffed, the cat sat in the open oven, its orange fur fluffed out by the residual heat from the previous night's cooking. One of my older cousins, who was experimentally minded, retrieved the carcass of a German incendiary from the roof gutters and filed down part of the casing, throwing the powder into the open part of the range. There was a satisfyingly blinding flash bigger than the brightest press photographer's bulb, followed by an eerie silence, before Jockie wiped his eyes with the back of his hand.

'So now we know,' he said.

'Now we know what?' Queenie shrieked.

'How the monkey come to see no evil.'

Jockie was so named for his size. The 1901 census has him as a printer's labourer but he must have been the least among his kind. In the Great War he served in a bicycle battalion, marching off to the Western Front with his bicycle at the trail. Somewhere in Flanders or France there was presumably a graveyard of abandoned bikes to match the B-17s in Cambridge. He slugged it out in the trenches, rolling Nosegays under parapets that must have seemed to him reassuringly high. He sang all the great songs of that war still, in a voice that sounded like a choking dog, for there was a perpetual ball of soot at the back of his throat that he could never properly expectorate. When he was in a good mood, he would take me out with a bucket and shovel to scrape up horse droppings for his matchbox-sized garden, disposed between the back wall of the parlour and the mangle shed. Next to it was the khazi, where a nightlight floated on a saucer of water.

His wife was hardly any smaller than he, but like the old Queen, whom she was said to much resemble and from whom she derived her nickname, Alice was round and heavy, big-chested and imposing. As a child she had run up and downstairs in the houses of the great, located across the river, emptying slops and carrying coal, scraping dog shit from the carpets and boiling water for the toffs to shave and bathe. The dialogue between these two cockneys is easier for me to remember now than things I may have said or heard last week. They had the glamour – and timing – of music-hall comedians.

'Look at his bleeding ribs,' Queenie observed on one of my extended visits from Cambridge. 'He looks no better than a skinned rabbit.'

'Nothing wrong with rabbits.'

'You could hang him up outside the butcher's and no one'd know the difference. What's that Squibs think she's up to?'

It was my mother's family nickname. I already had the knack of lying through my teeth.

'We had mince last week, Nan.'

'*Mince?*' she cried, as though I had confessed to eating hedgehogs out in the woods.

These examinations of my health would take place while I stood in a tin bath, the doors to the kitchen range open, my skin lathered with carbolic soap. The same soap, shaved into feathery slivers and added to a bucket of hot water, was used to wash the floor.

'What's more,' Nan said more than once, 'she's only gone and combed his hair in a girl's parting.'

'Nothing wrong with his spout, though,' Jockie countered, pointing.

'Don't you listen to him,' she ordered, scrubbing me dry with a threadbare towel.

On the first-floor front was a Victorian drawing room, furnished with an Indian carpet, a huge three-piece suite and other bits and pieces bought from market stalls. It was hardly ever used and in winter as cold as an icebox. Jockie and Queenie slept next door to it, under mounds of bedding. At the top of the house were two more bedrooms, the one I slept in with a dramatic mossy stain decorating the ceiling. The map it seemed to depict revealed a winding river that ran diagonally into a vast inland sea. In places the plaster had fallen, revealing the laths, and these I imagined as fortified cities filled with Seaforth Highlanders, whose impressive cap badge was my proudest possession. I kept it wrapped in a scrap of green velvet, along with a cocoa tin of glass marbles.

My grandmother considered me lost to the real world, for she had raised boys who could make and mend anything. It amused her to see me reading a year's back issues of the *Daily Mirror*, which were stored on the treadle of an old sewing machine in the passage between the shop and the parlour; or plucking hopefully at the remaining strings to the harp. To buck me up, Jockie gave me nails and scraps of wood to hammer together, much as one would occupy a hopelessly slow-witted asylum inmate.

They moved about the house with regal calm. The thin wooden door to the scullery would open daintily and Queenie would huff her weight up the one step to the parlour.

'Here we are,' she would announce gratuitously. When she sat, it was with a monarch's finality. In silhouette, Jockie would come down the passage from the shop with sparks flying from his roll-up, his shirtsleeves neatly folded back to his elbow, his boots creaking. He wore both braces and a belt, as though trousers were the sort of things likely to be snatched away by the lightest puff of wind. He liked to drag his chair sideways to the table and sit resting his head in the palm of his hand, his crossed legs revealing black socks over grubby combinations. Disposed like this, the two of them made a painterly conversation piece, though often nothing was said for an hour or so. The clock ticked, the trams clattered. On some nights the sirens went.

'Bollocks to that,' Jockie always said. In the heyday of the Blitz they had made the experiment of walking to Lambeth North tube station and waiting out the all-clear on the fuggy platform. I went with them a few times, not as awestruck as perhaps I should have been. A steady breeze came from the tunnels, rustling the sleeping forms, blankets drawn up over their heads to keep the grit at bay. Some families carried down a kitchen chair, where the head of the family would sit, smoking, or on which Ma would doze with a grandchild on her lap. It was not to Jockie's taste at all. Incendiaries had bounced off the roof of his house without setting fire to it: he felt lucky. Now, when the Germans were over London, he directed me to sit under the table with a torch from the shop to play with.

'What's it like down there in the cellar? Knock three times if you're asleep.'

He had an occasional job bundling up the *Evening Standard* with sisal string (of which we had several balls surplus to requirements) and then driving round the West End chucking the parcels out at street-corner vendors. Once in a while he came home late and, as he put it, aeriated. On one of these occasions, he staggered in, a canvas news-seller's bag on his shoulder.

'Yes,' Queenie yelled. 'And now you want your dinner, do you?'

She opened the oven and drew out a plate to which his scrag end and spuds stuck in carbonised lumps. She threw the sizzling mess the length of the passage and Jockie, swaying gently in the shop, opened the neck of the bag. His dinner disappeared inside as if directed by radar. With perfect timing, he hung the bag on the tyre rack and advanced on us with his arms out, like Captain Cook greeting the natives.

'What was that you just said, my beloved?'

On quiet rainy days I was allowed to climb into the shop window, carpeted with generations of dead flies, and rearrange the inch-high paper boxes indicating that we sold gas mantles, and then lay out, as for an anatomy lesson, the working parts of the bicycle. I sometimes spent the whole day in the window, crawling round like some bottled stick insect, knocking over with my feet what I had just erected with my hands. Queenie sat placidly peeling spuds in the parlour, or lay back in her chair, the cat clinging to the slopes of her lap.

'What do you fancy doing when you grow up then?' Jockie asked.

'Don't know.'

'Well, go on.'

'Perhaps I'll be a Seaforth Highlander.'

'That'll be just your bleeding cup of tea,' Jockie replied.

'What were you in the war, Grandad?'

'He ran a crown and anchor board,' Queenie answered.

43

'I was a sniper.'

'Did you kill anyone?'

'Yes, but I only shot them as had monocles.'

There was a war story I loved to hear. As he marched away to France from his depot, my grandmother took the trouble to come down from London to see him off, dragging with her the four boys. When she waved to him and coo-eed, his sense of military discipline did not permit him to respond. Queenie gave the children into the temporary care of a bystander, followed him down the road and, bursting into the ranks, punched him up the throat.

'Cobblers,' Jockie said, uneasy.

'As sure as I'm sat here.'

'That's it! Spit on the honour of the regiment. Was I or was I not a sniper? Answer me that.'

'No, you bleeding wasn't.'

The radio sat on a battered four-drawer chest stuffed with photographs of my father's side of the family, so that I could ask to look at 1920s pictures of Jockie in a stiff suit and a billycock hat, standing belligerently with the sea at his back; or Queenie in a white bonnet, one huge arm arranged along the sill of an open charabanc. Sometimes the location of these pictures was written on the back of the print in a childlike hand. The only photograph of my mother was taken on her wedding day. She wore a rented paste tiara and youth gave her empty expression a haunting beauty. There were no group portraits of the wedding and the image might as well have been captured in some country far from Lambeth. For many years it stuck in my mind as vaguely Russian.

'Do I have another Nan and Granpa?' I asked Queenie.

'Not that you'll ever see.'

'Are they dead in the war?'

'Eat your dinner,' she muttered.

In short, life was lopsided. What made sense in one house had no meaning elsewhere – for example, a photograph I showed them of myself standing in Elsie and Dick's patch of runner beans, dressed in an Aertex shirt and tartan tie, shading my eyes with my hand, left Queenie scowling and suspicious. There was too much sky in the story. Likewise the emotional warmth of life round the Walk, the games of brag and gin rummy, the lengthy conversations with the cat (at whom Queenie would sometimes wag a wooden spoon to make her point) had no place in Cambridge. My mother hated and feared her mother-in-law and I think this was a traffic that ran both ways. With Queenie there was a Sicilian understanding of honour: everything could be excused and forgiven provided it stayed within the family.

A dark secret seeped out. I had often noticed two white scars on my mother's breast, the shape of tears. Nobody told me how they came there but I found out by that most obvious of war-time indiscretions, careless talk. At some time when I was young enough to be in a pushchair my father had come across her kissing a man in the street – more accurately, in the passage that ran beside the Regal Cinema. He had beaten and kicked this poor devil unconscious and that night my mother plunged an open pair of scissors into her chest. She was sectioned with the help of a lazy or incurious doctor and sent to the asylum in Fulbourn.

This terrible story ought to have mattered more. When my grandparents laid their heads on the pillow at night I think they reflected that life was hard enough and what could not be easily incorporated into their comic routine was best left unsaid. Queenie did not like my mother and made no effort to understand or help her. It partly explains her complete silence touching my other grandparents, who were after all only a quarter of a mile away across the Lambeth Bridge Road. They too were consigned to outer darkness. I never met them – or if I did it was as a babe in arms. They paid the price of bearing a wicked daughter.

There was only one photograph of Queenie's grand-children in the entire house and it was of me, taken about the time my mother went away to the asylum. Hanging it in such a prominent position above the parlour table was a senti-mental gesture that concealed an ugly truth. I could be cherished and indulged but never again my mother. It was the downside of the love they bore me.

Altogether, what my parents were to each other before I was born is much less known to me than, for example, the early years of Queen Victoria, or the life of Thackeray. Relatives have told me since, in very guarded terms, that in his youth Bert wanted Ada with such a passion that nothing and no one else would do. There had been fisticuffs with a rival from the Borough Road, a butcher, before she relented and gave herself to my father. It is a story hard to believe, belonging to two other people altogether.

In the eyes of her in-laws – and her husband – my mother was mad. That she was bad flowed from the same source. She had to be tolerated because Bert was away fighting a war and, more than that, because I was in the world. Without me, she would probably have come out of Fulbourn Hospital and wandered away to live the rest of her life wherever she could. When she was in her seventies and living in the accumulated glories of my father's retirement, one of her schemes was to bunk off out of it all and sell flowers on Waterloo Station. If not flowers, she said, with a complete absence of irony, then lucky heather.

Jockie and Queenie had a pal in Brixton, the lugubrious Navvy Hall, who ran an off-licence. Once in a while we went by tram to see him, an adventure always signalled by Jockie shaving with an open razor, sharpened on a leather strap which had been cut from a Southern Railway window sash. His shaving brush was of the purest beaver, given to him, he claimed, by one of the crowned heads of Europe. He would submit to having me lather him like Father Christmas, gobs of white falling off his chin and on to his waistcoat, where he kept a cheap hunter watch.

'Don't take it up for a living,' he would mutter peaceably.

'Does shaving hurt?'

'Only when you cut your throat.'

'Have you ever done that?'

'More'n a few times.'

He shaved with the help of a rear-view mirror canni-balised from some cab. With this propped against the mantelpiece, he would parody the act of shaving, his nose pinched between trembling fingers.

'Ogorbli!' he would exclaim suddenly, staggering back-wards.

'Be careful, grandad,' I would howl.

'It's just the old war wound,' he invariably replied. 'Just the price of victory what the working man has paid for with his health. Eh?'

As he waved the razor about, Queenie watched him, her purple felt hat already on her head, the fruit decorating it dusty with age.

'Who needs Charlie Chaplin?' she would muse sourly, sipping a port and lemon.

At last Jockie would be ready, his cheeks a waxy red, a white silk muffler tucked into his melton overcoat. After the final brushing of his boots he habitually made a few passes over the lapels of this coat, so that they had gathered over the years a peculiar sheen. Then we would set off to the tram stop in the Kennington Road, all three of us holding hands. While my father was someone who came alive out of doors, strangers only made Jockie pugnacious. Clattering over the points by a pub called The Horns, hardly before we had started out, he would round on perfectly amiable fellow passengers and ask them who they thought they were looking at? We invariably went up the hill to Brixton with Jockie offering to square up.

'Come on then,' he would shout. 'You want it, do you? Then come and get it, you toerag.'

'You'd be better keeping him off the sauce, mother,' his opponents would advise, bewildered.

'Garn out of it! If I wasn't holding this kid here, I'd give you one meself.'

'Calling me pissed now is it?' Jockie would marvel, shaking his narrow head, glistening with bay rum. 'I tell you what, chum. You give me one more sideways look, and I'll be after you like shit off a shovel.'

'Blind-old-bleeding-Riley,' the conductor said when summoned. 'Don't you people know there's a war on?'

When we got to Effra Parade, these adventures would be recounted to Navvy Hall, who listened with a lowering expression, once in a while adding a point or two in his low, humourless voice, even more of a croak and summoned through curtains of phlegm.

'You done right, Harry,' he would conclude, his hand inching towards the pack of cards which would supply them with their entertainment. They sat at a table with an American oilcloth covering, betting in halfpennies and drinking stout, pausing only to complain loudly when the shop bell rang and some thirsty citizen stood revealed in the buttery yellow light.

'How's your Doreen's boy?' Navvy asked one of the regulars in his ruined baritone.

'He's in Burma.'

'Hot out there, is it?'

'He don't say. Who's this?'

'Bert's boy.'

'Harry and Alice in the back, are they?'

'Shove off,' Navvy chided. 'You ain't getting a drink, Arfer.'

As the man left, I explained that the man's name was not Arfer but Arthur.

'I call him what he calls hisself,' he replied, nettled.

'He don't mean no harm. It's his mother talking,' Queenie apologised. 'The silly mare.'

The Walk was everything to me. The earliest photograph of my father is of him and his brothers standing outside the shop, all of them barefoot and the youngest in a girl's smock. It can be dated to about 1912 but might have been taken any time in the previous thirty years. Much more than any public building, Number 15 has stuck in my mind as the quintessential London, hardly a step nearer modern times than the city Dickens explored on foot in *The Uncommercial Traveller*. A quarter of a mile away was Lambeth Palace, a rich source of political and ecclesiastical history, about which we knew only two things. One archbishop had donated land next door to the palace to make a park and recreation ground; another, Cosmo Lang, was commended locally for having stuck it out in the Blitz, sleeping in the so-called Lollards' Tower and being nagged to go down into the cellars when the sirens sounded. The palace was damaged in September 1940. Eight months later, in May 1941, a stick of four bombs landed in the courtyard and destroyed the Tower with Archbishop Lang inside it: he survived. But the real Lambeth was the semi-mythical purlieu of people like Old Moore and his almanac, Astley's Circus, and Ducrou, the nineteenth-century equestrian; or Richard Flixmore, the dancing clown. There were spa waters under the pavements of the Walk that went back to an even earlier age when, as Jockie explained to me, all the nobs walked about in syrup of figs.

'We had class then,' he said negligently, referring to a period in the eighteenth century when Lambeth Wells had enjoyed a brief ascendancy.

Our own place in history was cemented in 1937, when Lupino Lane opened *For Me and My Gal* at the Victoria Palace. Harry Lupino came from a hundred-year-old tradition of clowns and tumblers and his characterisation of Harry Snibson, the irrepressible flash cockney, fitted the idea we had of ourselves like a glove. The show tune – our understanding of what constituted the show tune – was 'The Lambeth Walk'. It includes the lines, 'Everyone's free and easy, do as you darn well pleasey.' This injunction went round the world. I last heard it at a family funeral in 2003, where it was featured as a farewell to Navvy Hall's daughter-in-law. Nobody thought its inclusion in the service the least bit unconventional, though as someone said darkly of the recording, 'That's not the Lupinos, it's that bugger Ambrose taking the piss.'

From the front door of this house in the Walk we had watched the scribbling of vapour trails in the air battles of 1940. That night, Queenie told me how she and the children – my father would have been exactly my age – had stood on the same doorstep and listened to the bombardment that preceded the trench assaults on the first day of the Somme offensive in 1916. It was, she said, like distant thunder. (My mother's memory of this same war was being sent to loot Jewish shops in the immediate aftermath of the Zeppelin raids, climbing through the shattered windows of traders with names like Goldstein and Blumgarten and snatching whatever there was left to steal.)

Jockie, veteran of what was known as the Gaspipe Cavalry, drank at home, though there was a pub a few yards away in China Walk: in some way or other, this choice placed us among the respectable poor. A nightly glass of stout or two while playing cards was not the same as soaking it up in the saloon bar. It makes him sound uncompanionable and perhaps he was. He had a pal in the Borough Road, another tiny Londoner. Jack Riach spent his days reading works from his own vast library, scratted together from market stalls, when eighteenth-century calf bindings could still be bought for a few pence. The first book I ever owned came from this source: Dr Johnson's Dictionary, the eighth edition, with a signature and the seal of the vice-consul's office in Dieppe.

Mrs Broom, the expert on matriculation, examined it with a scholar's care.

'Very good,' she pronounced. 'And useful too, I dare say.'

The huge valve radio was a modern addition, but the house retained its gas brackets, iron kitchen range, copper washtub and flagstone scullery. The pattern on the lino was of Victorian design, as was the etched glass in the door from the shop to the parlour. Grown-ups played cards on a dark green chenille cloth flung over a table made to last. In an alcove was a collection of odds and ends, including six beautifully engraved lager glasses liberated by Jockie from some ruined estaminet, he could not remember where. As a special treat, my grandmother would sometimes make me a milkshake from custard powder and lemonade. To this she would add a dollop of jam for flavour, whisk the mess vigorously in a saucepan and then serve the result in one of these glasses. It was satisfyingly disgusting.

'Up West' was the generic description of London across the water. Of the rest of England, my grandparents had been to Kent for summers spent picking hops, and Sussex on forays to the coast. The other shire counties (especially Cambridgeshire) were occupied by what they called swedes, slow-witted and clod-hopping people of no account. This disdain for others was general. In China Walk there was a grocer's run by a Welshman who had been there for many years. Nothing could persuade Jockie other than that this man came from a race cursed since Creation by shiftiness.

'You have a look,' he suggested. 'The eyes is set too close together.'

There was a bagwash a few doors down and a public baths on the corner of Kennington Road. It was here in 1924 that William Joyce, Birkbeck College student and youthful company commander of a movement called the British Fascisti, was slashed from mouth to ear in a bust-up with what he wanted to believe were Jewish communists. Joyce, who later became the infamous Lord Haw Haw, was convinced that his assailant had been trying to cut his throat. It seems much more likely that he was having his card marked by a local as an unwelcome interloper and (mistakenly) a bit of a toff into the bargain.

I remember the cubicles in this echoing place as being unusually generous and the baths frighteningly deep. While I watched my fingers pucker, Jockie would sit on the chair provided and read me bits out of the *Evening Standard* in a halting voice.

'"A Dalston man has grown a tomato that bears a striking resemberlance to Mussolini." Well, that ain't hard. You find a parsnip that looks like old Adolf, that's a story.'

Opposite us was a Rowton House, where Jockie assured me you slept upright and fully clothed with your arms tucked over a rope stretched from wall to wall. (This was a gross libel on the philanthropy of Lord Rowton, formerly Disraeli's private secretary and founder of this excellent charity for homeless men.) Lambeth Walk had been a street market for more than a hundred years, served by costermongers who stored their barrows down the side streets leading to 'The Arches', which supported the line into Waterloo. It was underneath these that we supposed Bud Flanagan to have composed his most famous song. At the far end of the Walk there was an eel-pie-and-mash restaurant and an Eyetie ice-cream parlour. There was a salvationist with a trumpet and a man without legs who scooted about on a little platform. Some way distant were the intimidating black gates of the bile bean factory, makers of a proprietary medicine to be found in every home round about.

There were a very few stories about my mother's childhood on the other side of the Lambeth Bridge Road. The best of these was how she, her sister Meg and a blind boy from Battersea used to play for street parties, when the pub gave up its piano to be carried out on to the pavement and the coster barrows were piled high to form barricades against the attentions of the police. Towards the end of her life I asked her who this boy was, and how he came to be involved.

'His name was George,' she said vaguely. 'He was at the same blind school as Meg.'

'Did he have a surname?'

Grumbling, she thought about it for a while.

'Shearing,' she said at last.

'You played the piano with *George Shearing*?'

'What, one of your pals, is he?' she said, stirring the last embers of derision.

'He's very rich and famous nowadays.'

'Like I'm Marie of Roumania.'

The greatest party ever held round at Queenie's was when my father and his youngest brother Jim happened to come home on leave together. Bert had flown back from India where he had been on some suitably hush-hush mission, delivering a general he was not at liberty to name. The implication was that Air Marshal Portal and the King had specially selected him for this work: a joke, but only half a joke. Receiving the King's commission and being mentioned in despatches to His Majesty had turned my father's head a little. Just as my mother had a *nom de guerre* (Peggy) that was not her given name, so Bert had transmogrified from the chippy Albert John to the more genial Tommy.

Jim had come home from North Africa with lance-corporal's stripes and tanned forearms. There were bananas and pomegranates and lengths of silk: the party was important enough to open up the upstairs parlour, which was haphazardly decorated with Christmas bunting. It is my recollection that all the family gathered that day. Certainly it was an occasion my mother could hardly refuse to attend and she sat with a smile pasted to her face, wearing a tight blue cotton frock and blocky high-heel sandals, her knuckles secretly white with fear.

'I am trusting you to keep your trap shut,' she whispered to me.

But I could tell from the general response to her plucked

eyebrows and painted legs that if the secret of how things stood in Cambridge was not already out, then suspicions were running dangerously high. My father glanced at her occasionally with barely concealed hostility, some of the heat from his glare warming my own face. There was a great deal of running up and down stairs, cutting of sandwiches and frying of chips. Jockie, who had once swum the Thames from Hungerford Bridge to Chelsea for a bet, whose party trick was – or had been – to eat a 78-rpm wax record or a plateful of buttons, was in his element. Overborne by heroic sons, he staggered about with a brown ale in his fist, muddling people's drinks and blowing fart noises through the tubes of a bicycle handlebar.

The highlight of the evening was Uncle Jim's sand dance, a concept fetched home from the desert, where he had been a fitter in a RAF fighter base. For this, Queenie had to be pushed upstairs like an over-stuffed sofa and enthroned on the Rexine couch. The rest of us were arranged in a circle round the extremities of the room. Before the performance began there were bouts of hysterical laughter and banging about on the stairs. During the Blitz there had been biscuit tins of sand on every floor of the house to extinguish incendaries, used by the cat when it was too wet to go outside. These were now carried in and the contents strewn on the Indian carpet, not without objections, and the scene was set for Jim's dance. Naked except for a see-through raffia skirt and two saucepan lids arranged as a brassiere, he twisted sinuously, a cigarette stuck to his lower lip. Leaning back to shake his non-existent belly fat, weaving his arms over his head, he could hardly dance for laughing. We screamed and clapped in unison.

That night I slept on the floor at the foot of my parents' bed. Jockie had given me more than a sip of brown ale and I was heated and faintly hysterical, with a blinding headache. A nightlight in a saucer of water illuminated the floor of the room for a few feet, though there was the beginnings of dawn in the sky outside. Downstairs they were singing. At about five in the morning my mother came bursting in, her hair down and the collar of her frock torn. She was barefoot.

'I told you to keep your effing mouth shut,' she screamed.

Chapter Three

THE WAR NOTWITHSTANDING, LONDON ALWAYS
seemed to me an area of greater safety than Cambridge. On
these visits to my grandparents, I could – and did – walk
across Lambeth Bridge and explore as far as the House of
Commons and Whitehall, a completely unregarded small boy
in a sea of uniforms and elderly cabs, horse drays and push-
bikes. I mooched along, not much more interesting than a
stray dog, staring at buildings about which I knew nothing.
Gales of grit blew, the air was thick with smoke and exhaust
fumes, cut by the occasional whiff of horse piss. I walked as
close to the gutter as I dared, an eye out for some treasure I
could take home to Jockie – a bolt, a bit of blackened hose,
perhaps an angle bracket in London Transport red livery. For
identification I carried my Seaforth Highlander badge. I was
never stopped or questioned, except once. A man in conversation with a colleague outside the Foreign Office gave me a
coin and asked me to nip down to the corner and buy him

the *Evening Standard*. When I came back, both men had disappeared. I took them to be German spies and threw the paper into a wastebin.

One way home was across Westminster Bridge and down the side of St Thomas's Hospital. By scrabbling with my toes and overreaching my arms I could peer over the Albert Embankment parapet at the Thames, then a sickly grey-brown colour, turbid with oil and flotsam. Coal barges were moored up in line astern. The backdrop – the Houses of Parliament – was just another public building. I did not know its name or function, any more than I knew the purpose of any of the Cambridge colleges.

On some of these visits to what I had falsely begun to think of as home, Jockie would take me to his barber, who had premises at the top of Kennington Road. There men his age and older would have the old hair-raid and piece out the news from the *Daily Mirror*. The room hung heavy with the scent of bay rum and steam from shaving towels wrapped round the cheeks and gizzards of some very decrepit old fight fans. The walls were decorated with boxer portraits, the most prominent of which was that of Bombardier Billy Wells. Wells came from the Mile End Road and was many times British Heavyweight Champion, his publicity photograph showing a lean and hungry-looking man in knitted black shorts. He was one of those spoken of in the boxing frater-nity as The Great White Hope.

'What does that mean?' I asked.

'Well,' one of the old men explained, 'you've heard of Jack Johnson, have you?'

'No.'

'Well, he was black, see? So he knocks out Burns, makes him heavyweight champion of the world, that's 1909. Now we wants someone to knock *him* out.'

'Did the bombardier do that?'

'No, mate,' he said sadly. 'Nor he never would have neither.'

'Why isn't there a picture of Jack Johnson on the wall?'

'Yeah, why is that, Sid?' the old man asked slyly of the proprietor.

In strictly practical terms, Cambridge was the safer place to be. In summer huge elms and chestnuts overhung the parks and men too old to be called up for military service played languorous games of cricket, or cycled home from allotments with bumper cabbages and baby-sized marrows. Their womenfolk tied up their hair in factory-girl scarves and, like the men, cycled everywhere. Even to my innocent eye, Cambridge people seemed healthier and more tanned than Londoners. They were less raucous and correspondingly more private. In Lambeth, Hitler-baiting was an art and the Führer's only means of locomotion, the goose-step, was something even the youngest child could imitate. In Cambridge, it seems to me now, there was much less ribaldry, at least among adults. Families who had given their sons and daughters to the war pedalled about in modest silence. From time to time they crossed the path of cycling policemen, red-faced and corpulent, their boots dusty with the roadway. I mentioned this comforting presence to Jockie.

'Never you mind that,' he muttered. 'Ever you see a copper, you cross to the other side of the road.'

'Is that what you do, Grandad?'

'He has to,' Queenie said.

One of my mother's unlikely skills was knitting – not the sort that goes with ticking clocks, cats and fireside radio shows but her own manic version, that went with chain-smoking and ear-burstingly loud dance music. Her practice was to buy sweaters from jumble sales for a few pence, have me unravel them and wind the wool, and then I would watch her flash away with the needles, referring from time to time to a torn pattern or two which she kept stored in the pages of the *Gardening Encyclopaedia*. She knitted for relaxation, I think, but once started would stay up all night. The evenings she went out she would sometimes give me a garment to unpick as a way of occupying my time. I would hurl the balls of wool about the room, bombing Berlin. Not everything she finished was as pictured on the front cover of the pattern.

'Stand up straight,' she would howl, tugging at me with vexed fingers.

'It's *pink*,' I blubbed.

'It is *not* pink, it is coral. There's kids in other parts of the world would give their eyeteeth for a pully like that.'

After a few cigarettes, she would relent.

'You're right. Unpick it.'

I wore grey flannel shorts – the same pair for weeks on end – and, I suppose, shirts, though I cannot remember one of them. In winter I wore a prewar gaberdine mac bought from a jumble sale, several sizes too big and a little on the green side of blue. It was set off (of course) by a knitted scarf in red-and-green stripes that reached to my knees. My mother encouraged me to wear the scarf wound round my neck in easy loops. As she pointed out, it looked nicer and in the event of frost could be used to cover the nose and ears.

It has often occurred to me that the true histories of who we were should have been written by the neighbours. On the other side of the partywall to our cacophony – the dance music, the slamming doors, Peggy's bouts of manic rage – lived a quiet, childless couple who must have had the forbearance of saints. He was exceptionally tall, a heavy man with soft blond hair and a raggy moustache. His wife was a tiny woman who worked as a bus conductress. She walked home in blue serge slacks peeping out from under a man's mac that reached almost to her ankles. If I was in the window, she would smile her frightened smile: if she saw the shadow of my mother in the room she would duck her head in terror.

Mr Pargeter was too gentle – translated by my mother to mean too soppy – ever to complain face to face. Instead, he pushed mildly worded notes through the letter-box after we had gone to bed. Peggy responded with notes of her own, one of them demanding to know why he wasn't in the army. I was in the garden one afternoon shortly afterwards when his face appeared above the boundary fence.

'Tell your mother I'm not in the army because – because –'

Then his face crumpled and he burst into tears. He rested his head on to his forearms, sobbing, before disappearing from view. When I told Peggy about this, she sat still for a few moments, examining the back of her hands. To my amazement, tears were welling in her own eyes.

The things in the house that were mine alone can be easily numbered. I had the Philip's Atlas, the book my father's crew sent me and Dr Johnson's Dictionary. It made good reading. *(SAL AMMONIAC is a volatile falt of two kinds. The ancient was a native falt, generated in inns where pilgrims, coming from the temple of Jupiter Ammon, ufed to lodge; who travelling upon camels, urining in the ftables, out of this urine arofe a kind of falt, denominated Ammoniac. The modern sal ammoniac is entirely factitious, and made in Egypt, with foot, a little fea falt, and the urine of cattle. Our chymifts imitate the Egyptian fal ammoniac by adding one part of common falt to five of urine, with which fome mix that quantity of foot.)*

In addition to these three books I had a cocoa tin of marbles and my Seaforth Highlander badge. I cannot remember pencils or paper. As for the baseball bat and ball donated by the USAAF, I took the bat across the field at the back of the house one guilty afternoon and threw it into the orchard

– or tried to. It landed on the far side of a drainage ditch and ending up leaning whimsically against a strand of barbed wire. The softball I kept hidden in a wardrobe drawer underneath an old and stained eiderdown. I liked its strange size and the raised welts of its seams. It was a new ball but seemed to me to carry a faint whiff of sweat about it, as though foretelling its destiny.

Meg, the blind aunt who had attended George Shearing's school, was now at a convent in Liverpool, from where she sent cheery Christian messages in Braille. My mother banged out bad-tempered replies with a machine presumably provided by a charity: Meg's letters she gave to me, out of a superstitious unwillingness to throw them away. They were practically the only correspondence we received. The bedroom floor was littered with them, curled like parchment. It was her idea that I could do something with them.

'You could make a paper aeroplane,' she suggested.

'Or a battleship, eh?'

'I can't think of nothing more easy.'

I had no way of knowing whether how we lived was normal. For all I knew, Mr Pargeter was crying for shame because he had a Tiger tank hidden in his back garden. I had never seen inside a single house or garden in the whole of Cambridge. The irresistibly glamorous version of Peggy with her pageboy haircut, her Cuban heels and chiffon scarves found her no more friends than the drab that played the radio loud enough to be heard in the street. A few middle-aged men would raise their stained trilbies hopefully as we walked to the bus-stop. My mother ignored them with a film star's disdain.

In Lambeth Walk and 295 Squadron there was an image of our life together that had Peggy forever living it up like a tart, flaunting her long legs and smoking her hat off while I sat at home, cowed and beaten. In fact, the reckless days were coming to an end. My mother still went out of a night, as she put it, but only to dance with her friend Kath, whose husband had been a Spitfire sergeant-pilot killed in a mid-air collision early in the war. She came home early: and very often, depressed. When the worst of these moods afflicted her, she would take to her bed for two or three days, neither eating nor speaking and getting up only when I was asleep, turning day to night and back again.

Of the two mothers, I much preferred the glamorous temptress. Dressed to kill, Peggy was exciting, even enchanting. Once, she was on the point of leaving the house when, remembering that she wore no knickers, she fetched some in from the garden clothesline and dried them in front of the gas oven. Then, turning her back on me she hoisted them up breezily before patting her skirt straight.

'That should keep the draught out,' she said.

Once in a while I would help her empty her handbag and brush out all the loose powder and bits of silver paper with my fingers before reassembling her lipstick, compact, comb and door key. There should have been a grey-green identity card in there too but she balanced being arrested and fined for not carrying it against the possibility of giving the wrong address and so confounding the hounds of hell that lay in wait round every corner. The last thing to go in was her purse, seldom with more than a few shillings in it.

The practically wordless slattern that replaced this shining image frightened me. Then, her clothes were strewn on the bathroom floor or in the bedroom and cups of tea I carried up to her would stay untouched. It was a fixed thing with us that she was the only person permitted to answer the door, a rule she dinned into me again and again. When she had given up on life, therefore, a knock would sound and whatever I was doing, in whatever room I was, I would freeze. Maybe it would be repeated – a gasman, a charity worker – but I knew enough not to betray by the smallest noise that inside this house there lived two people, one deaf and depressed, the other her ten-year-old minder.

When I was in charge of the house in this way, I had the uneasy feeling that when I went into a room, I was not really there at all, but seeing it through the eyes of an ant, or a moth. It was not mine to occupy in the ordinary sense, any more than would be a railway waiting room at midnight, or a deserted barn out in the Fens. The curtains to the front room were seldom drawn back and sunlight had reduced them to brittle rags. Their peppery smell pervaded the atmosphere, helping to create the illusion of an underground cave, or the entrance to a rabbit hole. There was a light switch but no bulb. Ancient embers overflowed the grate. A mirror over the fireplace was blinded by a pearly film of dust and grime. The clock had stopped at ten past four.

In the dining room, where of course we had never dined, there were no curtains at all. Late-afternoon sun would inch along brownish wallpaper. I carried in the blue-and-black rag rug and laid it by the french windows, the better to sprawl and play marbles. Earwigs occasionally wriggled through the gaps in the woodwork and darted under the curling lino. Apart from the table and chairs there were only two decorations in that room – a Clarice Cliff rabbit that had perhaps been a wedding present and a cut-glass fruit bowl which contained a torch powerful enough to signal to Mars if it hadn't been broken.

No milk or bread was delivered – there were shops for that a quarter of a mile away with prewar enamelled-tin advertising plaques illustrating, in one instance, a pipe-smoking man and his cheery spouse. He was sitting in a green chintz chair reading a newspaper, his head slightly thrown back in exclamation at some winning remark of his wife. Another of the plaques that never failed to intrigue me advertised Colman's Mustard. Impossibly plump sausages, done to a turn, lay waiting on a shiny plate. I took both these images – the happy couple and the sausages – to be statements of fact about an age gone by, perhaps never to return.

We lived in the kitchen, heated by the gas stove and lit by a naked electric light bulb. Without knowing it, I was colluding in my mother's desire for self-abasement: she was in fact a very good cook but we ate like impecunious students or railroad hobos because we didn't deserve and did not believe in anything better. Between us we drank oceans of tea poured from a brown betty with a ruined rubber spout – and gabbed. It was her word for idle conversation.

'Where's Venezuela, then?' she interrupted me once.

'It's in the atlas.'

'What'd they do there for a laugh?'

'It's hot.'

'You're not unhappy, are you?' she asked abruptly. 'I mean, you don't go round saying you're miserable to anyone you meet outside? I don't want none of that.'

For her, outside meant not simply the view from the door but all authority, an unmapped area where men – of course they would be men – sat in judgement over her. She was extremely uneasy if I left the end of the road and travelled by bus anywhere, which happened seldom enough. The sharp point of her concern was not that harm might come to me but that, in my innocent way, I would rat on her to a man who might be a mad doctor or a council nosy parker. (The only time an incident of this kind happened to me on the bus was when a poor blustering fool of a man stroked my hair and asked me home to tea. My terror was real enough to make him jump up and leave, his face brick-red, his flies wide open.)

My father, who had at least visited me once in New Malden, never came to Cambridge and did not write. On the face of it, his absence was no more remarkable than many another serviceman's and since I had no point of comparison, I supposed that all the homes with fathers at the war were more or less like ours. Whatever was wrong with us could only be put right by peace. The blocked toilet we cleared with a wooden coat hanger and a fearsome tin of caustic soda; the absence of hot water in the bathroom; ants running everywhere in the larder; the weekly purchase of a copy of the *Daily Express* to make into lav paper – all these things would disappear overnight when the war ended and the heroes returned.

There was an advertisement that seemed to promise this, one that I first noticed in a jumble-sale copy of *Wide World*, a magazine for men who liked to read stories about Dyak canoes gliding through mangrove swamps or Canadian Mounties hunting renegade trappers. In the copy that ran beneath a line drawing of himself, an explorer tells us that when revisiting an abandoned camp out on the Antarctic ice, he discovered a tin of Barney's Punchbowle Tobacco. To his astonishment and pleasure, it smoked as fresh as the day it was packed. Whoever wrote this ad was a genius, for it implied that what is lost can be found and that pleasure is uncorrupted by time. It was exactly what I wanted. I wanted someone to come home and save my mother.

One afternoon when she was feeling chipper, she took me to Joe Lyons in Petty Cury for a cup of tea and a piece of wan-looking apple pie. In a glass display cabinet were plaster of Paris examples of the ice-cream sundaes we might have ordered in happier times. They were grey with dust. There were a few leery-looking soldiers about but the majority of people there were women, several of them with fox furs and hats shaped like shoes. My mother gave them a derisive shufti.

'Old bags,' she muttered.

'Do Yanks come here?'

She studied me with dangerously pale eyes.

'No they don't. And no more do I, except to keep you quiet. Got it in for the Yanks, have you?'

But the question had been innocent. I changed the subject by showing her how you could look into a cup of tea and see your eye reflected on the water.

'Water is right for this gnat's-piss,' she agreed, lighting her third cigarette.

Waiting for the bus home, I saw a model yacht in a shop window, an exquisitely detailed prewar toy for some rich child. It was on display in what in those days was called a gents' outfitters. I vaguely associated it with the richly glistening sausages in the Colman's ad and, on an impulse, I asked Peggy to buy it for me. She went white with rage.

'That's it!' she cried, spit flying from her mouth, shaking me by the shoulders, her voice loud enough to be heard on the other side of the road. 'I got all the bloody money in the world of course. Who do you think you are? D'you think you're bleeding royalty or something?'

'Don't talk to him like that,' a man objected, very unwisely. She rounded on him.

'And you can keep your nose right out of it! I'll talk to him any way I like, you four-eyed git!'

The man backed off, blushing. Though he too had been waiting for the bus to arrive, he turned on his heel and walked slowly away down the pavement.

'See what you done now?' my mother bellowed at me.

When the chubby single-decker came she gestured me to the front and sat behind, fuming. My lip wobbling, I studied an ad (*Idris when I's dry*) that was screwed to the bulkhead separating the driver from his passengers. When I looked round, she was gone. Peering through the oval back window I could see her as a dot in the distance, walking down the hill towards the bus. I got off at our usual stop and sat down with my back to a garden fence, my head cradled in my arms, feeling light-headed. It was the first time I realised that she was not always in control of herself, not just at home, but everywhere.

At last she caught up with me and I scrambled to my feet. We walked home in single file. When we got in, she sat at the kitchen table, sawing the edge with the bread-knife, tears running down her cheeks and gumming up her mascara. It was no more than mid-afternoon, though without clocks we took our time from the radio and, by experience, the quality of the light in the sky.

'Go to bed,' she muttered in a matter-of-fact way.

'I'm sorry, Mum.'

'Wash your face, brush your teeth and go to bed.'

'Are you going out later?'

She pointed the bread-knife at me.

'Now I'm warning you. Don't start.'

About midnight, she woke me up. Using the bread-knife, she had carved a fluffy white hull from a damp log of firewood, rescued from a puddle outside the back door. The masts were made from metal knitting needles heated over the gas ring and plunged into the wood in a more or less straight line. She put this crude yacht into my hands and walked out without a word. The slam she made with the bedroom door shook the house.

Whose idea had it been to send me from the wreckage of Elsie's home to a small – a very small – boarding school near Fenner's cricket ground? The answer has to be my father, I think, though I can't imagine what advantage he thought he was securing for me. There were perhaps a dozen boarders, half of whom were very young children, and slightly fewer day boys and girls, of whom I was one. The building stank of cabbage and urine, some of it contributed by a cat called Xerxes, the rest by bewildered infant boarders, penned up on the first floor of what had once been a comfortable Victorian house. Huge laurels hid the property from the main road, so that we could hear but not see American convoys trundling past. What could be seen was the clock on the Catholic church, its minute hand dragging us through a school day that left us bored and stupefied.

The proprietor of this place was a gangling old man with the cares of office sitting heavily on his narrow shoulders. He wore a gown over an ancient suit, smoked furiously, and was prone to outbursts of rage in which he seemed to speak in tongues, though I have realised since that he was quoting snatches of Latin poetry to harden his point. He taught on any subject that took his fancy. On one occasion we walked to the fields behind the Leys School for a botany lesson. He plucked a buttercup and shouted to us, 'Look, children, *Ranunculus bulbosis*. Remember the name, for it will come in useful one day, to be sure.' Bending to search for something else to identify, he broke wind in a long grumbling drumfire, and when we sniggered, looked at us upside down from between his legs, his wild hair lit by the sun, his spectacles flashing. 'Thunder in the air, I think.'

His assistant was an Indian. Mr Banarjee spoke in a wonderfully lulling voice, hypnotically low and quiet. He was small, with tiny hands and feet, and seemed to me impossibly old. He taught elementary maths, disguised as anecdotes.

'Johnny has been sent by Mummy to buy some apples. He has a half-crown and the cost of those apples is tuppence a pound.'

'Is this in India, sir?'

'He buys four pounds –'

'Mummy must love apples –'

'She is making jam,' Mr Banarjee countered smoothly. 'Tell me please, what change does Johnny bring home?'

'It depends, sir.'

This from Armstrong, a huge red-faced boy with a shock of almost white hair. Banarjee studied him as though he were an interesting beetle, or a caterpillar.

'You are a very foolish fellow, Armstrong.'

'Sir, I was meaning to ask you about something else: do you know the difference between a letter-box and an elephant's bum?'

'Oh dear, dear, dear. You really must try to do better than that.'

I had the feeling that I was there, along with Armstrong, for being what the headmaster called 'a slow boy'. It was a phrase I overheard him using in a whisper to a parent – not about her own child, for that would never do – but some other luckless pupil. It is just possible that there was method in the Head's madness and that we were all being raised according to some arcane educational principle to do with retardedness. We ate woolly potatoes with the skins on 'because all the goodness was in the skins' and whale meat because whales had, the way the Head explained it, joined the war effort against Herr Hitler. Ask any British general the secret of military victory: it was regular bowel movements.

Mr Banarjee was altogether less strident. He lived on the premises with the designation of housemaster and was wheeled out when parents came to the school to consider enrolling their child. It helped that he was always to be seen with several books under his arm and when called upon to write anything, uncapped a tortoiseshell fountain pen with the delicacy of a Somerset Maugham, whom (I see now) he a little resembled. He wrote in mauve ink, the tip of his tongue peeping from his lips.

The headmaster's daughter also taught. She shared her father's height and his wild and wiry hair and had the unconscious habit of pushing her hand inside her blouse and fondling the top part of her breast. Her manner was languid in the extreme. She taught me how to shade a cone to give it solidity and what perspective meant. She gave these lessons whilst yawning and smoking. Some hugely anticipated afternoons she would paint her toenails red, showing surprisingly beefy thighs and a glimpse of coffee-coloured camiknickers.

'Is it true, Miss, that Hitler has only got one ball?' (Armstrong)

'Seems likely enough,' she murmured absently.

'What about Goebbels?'

At last she looked up.

'You are a pimple, Armstrong.'

'Thank you, Miss.'

'You will grow up to be a fat red-faced butcher or something like that. With blood under your fingernails and turds on the heel of your shoe.'

She levelled him with an unsmiling stare.

'You'll like that, of course.'

There were books in the school, broken backed editions of *Ivanhoe, Hereward the Wake* and the Temple series of Shakespeare's plays, their bindings shattered. Mr Banarjee coaxed us through *A Midsummer Night's Dream,* a text as foreign to us, most of us, as *The Upanishads.* I had of course never seen a play performed and the stumbling, mumbling recitation we brought to the job was like wandering about in a pitch-dark forest, unlit by moonlight.

'He is your greatest poet,' Banarjee objected in his mild way.

'I hope I never meet him,' Armstrong said.

But I knew enough to know that this was Armstrong's incurable whimsy. Shakespeare was not only dead, but old. Bombardier Billy Wells was old (though in actual fact he was still alive and did not die until the 1960s) but he at least had some connection with the present, as represented by my grandfather. This Shakespeare was just a name on the title page, an ancient and faintly malign ghost, conjuring boredom and vexation. What was written on the page stayed stubbornly on the page.

As for our own self-expression, this was done with wooden pen-holders and rusting nibs on loose scraps of lined paper. These were handed in at the end of the lesson and seldom seen again, though the headmaster's termly reports indicated percentage achievement in individual subjects, some of which had never been formally taught. In this way I came top of history for an essay on the First World War, drawn exclusively from Jockie's reminiscences. It read, in its entirety: *When the call came, the British Army got on its bicycles and set off to war. My grandfather was a sniper at the time. His medals were lost in the post.*

One day, my father came to the school, wearing uniform with a flight lieutenant's insignia. He said a few words to the secretary and then walked outside to stand by the laurels, smoking a cigarette with the manly dash I remembered. The headmaster bounded into the classroom to interrupt Banarjee on the power of the monsoon and gave me an exeat, as he put it, with an over-genial wave of his arm. He was only too glad to get rid of us – generally the arrival of a parent was the prelude to harsh words and loss of income. Father and son met on the crumbling stone steps and walked through the fields to Grantchester more or less in silence. Once there, we sat outside the pub, which was shut. I asked him about the conduct of the war.

'Walls have ears,' he replied. He lit his pipe and pushed the spent match into the grass. When he saw me watching, he explained, 'If everyone did that, we wouldn't have the problem of matchsticks everywhere. Look round you, look at the floor. People don't care any longer. Anything goes.'

'When are you coming home?'

'Abso-bloody-lutely,' he said, with a short bark of laughter. 'You know they want me stay in?'

'After the war?'

'Yes,' he said. He smoothed away some crumbs from the tin table we sat at.

'Will you stay in?'

'The war isn't over yet.'

He was nervy. Having buried his match, he knocked his pipe out on the leg of the table, scattering black goo.

'They seem decent enough people at the school, the school you're at.'

I had never heard the adjective applied in this way.

'I hate it there.'

'Don't talk like your bloody mother. What is there to hate?'

I felt the tears springing into my eyes.

'You're not getting bullied, are you?' he asked.

'No.'

'You want to stick up for yourself more. You're too timid. What's nine nines?'

I was terrified.

'We haven't done that yet.'

'Well, get your finger out. You should *know*. You can't sit round half asleep all day long. What would ten nines be?'

'I don't know.'

'Would be ninety. Well, nine short of that.'

'Eighty one,' I muttered after a long pause, my face burning.

He pushed his iron chair away and stood up.

'We better get weaving. But listen to me. You've got to pull your finger out. You're not a kid any more.'

I was nine. It came to me in a flash that we were having this conversation outside a village pub that was closed because he had not wanted to walk into Cambridge and meet my mother by unlucky accident. His real anger had nothing to do with the nine times table. We tramped back across the fields by the side of the Cam where currents stirred long fronds of weed. Though I had never been on the river, it was well known that some that fell into it never returned to the surface.

'Not quite true,' Mr Banarjee told me once when I asked him about this.

'How, sir?'

'Most things come back to haunt us,' he said absently.

That day, my father walked with his hands in his pockets, taking them out only on the approach of some other rambling figure. He was, after all, not representing himself in these chance encounters but an officer in His Majesty's armed forces. If the person who was coming towards us was of sufficient importance, he gave him a cheery hello and a few shouted words about the weather. In this way we met an elderly and donnish-looking man, carrying an umbrella and – glistening and impossibly juicy-looking – a cabbage in a string bag.

'Is this your boy?' he asked, beating my father to the greeting.

'This is the sprog,' the flight lieutenant replied jovially.

'And how's the war going?'

'Don't ask me what I can't tell you.'

'Does that mean you don't know?'

'It means you can sod off,' my father replied.

His visit left me with much to think about, chief of which was whether to tell my mother. I did not. At school, I told them that he had taken me to tea at the University Arms and when that did not impress, added that he had bought me an airgun. Armstrong eyed me speculatively. According to him, *his* father was a commando who knew seventeen ways to kill a man with his bare hands. Sergeant Armstrong's military service was so secret that he had not been home since 1943. He could be anywhere. I had actually met Mrs Armstrong at what passed for the school sports, held on Parker's Piece. She seemed an unlikely wife for a killer commando, painfully thin and with arthritic hands. She wore a defeated-looking beaver coat that took all her strength to support.

'Are you one of Stuart's chums? she asked plaintively. 'You do seem a very nice little boy, I must say. Such lovely floppy hair.'

The book my father's crew had given me was *The Little Grey Men* by 'BB', first published in 1942. It tells the story of the last gnomes left in Britain, who live close to nature with only the fox, the stoat and human beings as their enemies. When the book opens, one of them, Cloudberry, has set off to find the source of the Folly Brook and the other three follow after to find and perhaps rescue him. My father himself could never have chosen this story, which is written in a high style and, though very dramatically shaped, requires both a great degree of literacy and an unquestioning love of the country-side. 'BB', the pen name of Denis Watkins-Pitchford, has sometimes been described as a sporting author – he was a keen shot and a dedicated carp fisherman – but his genius was expressed in the evocation of a very English (and now almost extinguished) landscape. In his story, the last gnomes in Britain are not to be found in Wales or the West Country, but in Warwickshire.

The most memorable part of the journey along the Folly is the discovery of an abandoned Basset Lowke model of a coastal steamer, correct in every detail, which the gnomes use to help them on their way. An adult reading of the book reveals a startling shift in scale from chapter to chapter, so that, for example, in one scene Dodder, Baldmoney and Sneezewort cook their fish in the lid of an old cocoa tin, in another in the brass cap of an expended cartridge. But, however improbable, sailing and living on this model ship was for me the essence of high adventure. 'BB' quite bril-liantly evoked the wish of every child to shrink to occupy his favourite toy. What the kingfisher had to say about life, no matter how amiable the squirrels, voles, hedgehogs and assorted wildlife, the part of the book I understood best was the discovery of the *Jeanie Deans* and sailing her by clockwork motor across the vast waters of an inland sea, in reality the ornamental lake of some long established country house.

The landscape out towards Cherry Hinton had something at least of gnome country about it. There was a riven oak, in which I could hide; a few streams supporting minnows; banks of cow-parsley and willow herb; in summer, clouds of butterflies. I had the townie's anxiety about crossing fences and was generally a very unadventurous explorer, though with an excellent sense of direction. From time to time there were human mysteries to be puzzled over: for example, an elaborately carved heart pierced by an arrow cut into the trunk of a tree; in another place a rotting wallet with a photograph of an elderly woman tucked inside it. Much more obvious was the camp set up for Italian POWs, barely under guard at all. Men in vests played bowls with great rounds of wood they had fashioned themselves, or sunbathed between the huts. All this meant more to me, I am ashamed to say, than any impulse from a vernal wood. I shared with 'BB' what I took to be the essential melancholy of life in the wild. Even on sunny days, the wind soughing in the branches or the eerie emptiness of forsaken pastures could send me running until my ribs ached.

Armstrong had mastered the male erection – that is to say, he had not mastered it at all but was in thrall to it. Practically everyone in school had seen the tortured evidence, poking from the fly of his trousers. Armstrong's expression when he gave these exhibitions was a mixture of pride and something else, a sort of shamed anxiety. In his ox-like way, he seemed to believe that only he was afflicted with this terrible ache. It was annoying for him to discover that a much smaller boy, the black-eyed and tousle-haired Page, could, by vigorous chafing, achieve the same effect. And so, we found, could we all. There began an almost medieval frenzy of self-abuse, only quelled by the intervention of the headmaster. He summoned all boys to the largest classroom and kept us waiting in the charge of Banarjee for twenty minutes or so.

When he came in, it was with his daughter in tow – either a careless oversight or (more likely) an exquisite form of additional torture. By ruthless question and answer, while the dust danced in the afternoon sunshine and the Head paced between the desks, Armstrong was identified as the leader of our grubby little investigations, as they were described.

'I do wonder what that poor woman your mother would make of all this, Armstrong,' the Head boomed, fluffing out his gown. 'Is it your wish that I should tell her? I have only to pick up the telephone. Advise.'

'I won't do it again, sir.'

'Ha! Wonderful!' his tormentor bellowed, throwing back his head and exposing his yellow smoker's teeth in genuine mirth. His daughter studied her nails. Mr Banarjee turned a page of the book he was covertly reading and smoothed it down with his tiny brown hand. Poor Armstrong. He sat at a rickety desk with his sausage thighs bursting from his shorts, sweat running down his face. He looked hunted. There was a cattle market a mile away where I had once seen a bullock break loose from the pens and attempt to make a run for it. The expression in its eyes when it was cornered was not unlike Armstrong's.

I remember this incident so well because it was the first time I had ever asked myself why people could be easily cowed and bullied by fools and scoundrels. I did not have the words to express it in just that way, but there was something very ugly about a dozen boys being harangued by an old man we all thought dippy, without any of us daring to move a muscle. It seemed to me – and these words did fly into my mind at the time – that the Head was enjoying himself. It was like being in a film about the infinitely cruel and silky-voiced Nazi colonel, whose job it was to interrogate the captured patrol. In purely physical terms, Armstrong was big enough to have made a run for it. Young as he was, had it come to racing to the door and doing a bunk down Hills Road, he could have made it without difficulty. His father would not have hesitated: it was just the sort of thing commandos excelled at. The son could have crept on to a London train, locking himself in the lavatory compartment until the coast was clear. Once at Liverpool Street, it was simply a case of melting away into the crowds and sleeping rough in the bomb sites round St Paul's.

Instead, and to my horror, the terror of the school began snivelling. It broke the spell of a terrible fantasy I had begun to harbour, in which the hero of the adventure was neither Armstrong nor his father, but myself.

Then, incredibly, abruptly, the war and all the misunderstandings it had generated came to an end. On VE night, the advertising hoardings at the corner of the road were torn down and burned, sending sparks flying upwards into the damp and smoky air. The picture of a man and wife cycling into the future with their child gave itself up to the flames like paper. A querulous old man stood at his gate and pointed out that what we were doing was illegal. He was roundly jeered. There was an almost animal release that night: something wonderful and unrepeatable was taking place, fuelled by bottled beer, wild singing and a good deal of exuberant kissing. It happened that a sailor was home on leave and though nobody much liked him or the family he came from, this local hero was given twenty-two birthday bumps in the trampled grass. He was so drunk that when he was let go, he lay on his back like a dead man.

Well after midnight, people stood talking to each other in their front gardens, or walked up and down the pavements, their faces prised apart as much by shock as joy. Many front doors stayed open, giving glimpses of interiors never before seen. Flags hung from bedroom windows – the Union Jack, of course, but also those of France, Australia and in one baffling instance, Brazil. There were the distant sounds of thunder flashes and fire-engine bells, and the occasional eruption of a faraway football crowd roar, the kind that greets the home team's goal.

I ate fish-paste sandwiches and dry homemade tarts served from card tables set up outside people's houses, and swigged dandelion and burdock from a flagon bottle. From the posh side of the street, a woman had planted Chinese lanterns on the grass verge and there was music – of a sort – provided by a portable gramophone operated by her bearded husband. We made peace to Gilbert and Sullivan.

'You never say hello to me,' a serious and tubby girl with plaits and spectacles said to me in the gloom.

'When?'

'On the bus.'

'Well, you never say hello to me.'

'My mother says you're common.'

I stared at her. She was wearing a school mackintosh buttoned up to the chin and a fawn scarf worn like a shawl, crossed over her chest and tucked into the belt at the back. At that moment the sailor was being carried past by two elderly men. This girl – she was called Gloria – wrinkled her nose. It made her spectacles wink.

We walked home in company with her parents, an amiable father with even crueller glasses than his daughter, and my accuser, Mrs Wilkes.

'Aren't we all up late?' she trilled. 'And where's your mother tonight, dear?'

The answer was: in the kitchen, smoking. She looked up,

bleary-eyed. When I offered to make her tea, she nodded miserably. We sat at opposite ends of the narrow kitchen table, in the sort of silence that comes to old married couples. The secrets we shared had become historic items. Somewhere, in some unimaginable place, my father was presumably greeting the peace in his own way, his pigeon-blue eyes darting this way and that as the boys let their hair down. But we had a little history of our own that had not included him and which had suddenly run up on to the rocks with a shattering crunch.

My mother wiped her nose with the back of her wrist and lurched off to bed. I turned off the gas oven, stood on tiptoe to bolt the back door, put the cups into the sink, and followed after. In the goods marshalling yards, shunting engines sounded their whistles, with an effect that was more of a warning than any celebration.

Chapter Four

AS WITH A GREAT MANY MEN OF HIS GENERATION, the war gave my father an education in social opportunity. He rose from the ranks, grasped the significance of that new phenomenon, a meritocracy – and learned how to exploit it. Slips pasted into his flight logbook showed consistently above-average marks in all tests and certainly he took part in some hair-raising daylight operations, among others towing gliders at D-Day, Arnhem, and the crossing of the Rhine. He was that most envied and desirable of airmen, the unflappable heavy bomber navigator with a reputation for bringing the boys home.

The most important thing to him was his commission and its consequences: he finished his service in triumph as instructor to the Empire Air Navigation School. All that pipe-smoking and public jocularity had paid off. He was not yet forty, was if anything even more dashingly handsome in appearance and had developed a ruthlessness that begged to be employed. When he was discharged from the RAF, he discovered that what he wanted from life and what was there to take had aligned themselves like benign planets.

He did not come home to the Cambridge Telephone Exchange, with its sleepy social club and provincial city mentality. Cambridge had doubled in population between the wars and it was that opportunity which brought us there in the 1930s. But the thirties were now a very old story. The big chance lay in London, in the smoky streets and newly unbandaged public buildings across the river from Lambeth. The sandbags and the timber shoring disappeared, miles of paper tape were peeled back from office windows and reconstruction beckoned. It called for an unsentimental outlook and dedicated hard work. These were aboriginal gifts in my father and the times suited him perfectly. He lodged first with his mother in Lambeth Walk, then with a brother in Kentish Town, and set about winning the peace from an engineering planning department in Great Titchfield Street, on the edge of literary Fitzrovia.

Whatever was happening round about held no interest for him. He was one of those who marched past some famous and notorious pubs in a suit and tie, pipe jutting, sturdy shoes clapping out a rhythm on the pavement, a man with a man's work to do. The former telephone linesman wore a RAF Association scarf, a heavy grey overcoat and the first of a long series of brown trilbies. He gave the civilian world his burly truculence, signed off papers with a beautifully assertive signature, blanked the weak and venal. In shops, buying his cigarettes, he would proffer his money and at the same time specify the change he was to receive. For relaxation he read *Wireless World.* When the BBC restored its television service, he scratch-built a receiving set for Queenie, soldering together war surplus equipment on the shop bench in Lambeth Walk. The picture was got from a six-inch screen, coloured green, such as he had used sitting at a navigator's desk in a shuddering Stirling: airborne radar turned to a more frivolous use.

These were my first glimpses of him as he saw himself. The Walk could hardly contain him now and his brusque RAF manners must have startled his parents and dismayed his brothers. There was a daemon lurking behind all that confected jollity. In politics he was a working-class Tory, with a fine disdain of lefties, commies, poofs, conchies, spivs, scroungers, tarts and of course, above all, Yanks. The French were gutless, the Italians pitiable, the Spanish more akin to gipsies than anything else. The Jocks could be tolerated for their qualities of courage and lippiness but there was never a kind word to be had from him about the Taffs. Paddies were treated with indulgence, the way simple-minded people are. Though he did not know it, the more dangerous political virus that he carried with him, that would in the end find him out, was a raw and unbalanced hatred of what he called 'clever sods' – the educated minds who ran enterprises like the BBC or the Foreign Office. In sum, he was a not uncommon example of a very, very gifted man without a real idea in his head.

All of which was for the moment beside the point. What mattered was that his postwar plans left my mother and me firmly anchored in Cambridge. In what fateful conversation did he tell her that her lot was to stay exactly where she was? They were both Londoners, of course, but for her it was more of a state of mind than a birthplace. She was a slum kid who never grew up. When I think of her now it is as a skinny-legged child climbing out of a shattered shop window, clutching nothing more valuable than a loaf of bread or a tin of peas. She was a figure running away from the sound of police whistles and nothing that happened to her later could change any of that. For all that she knew or cared, Cambridge might as well have been Kidderminster or Kirkcaldy. It was not London. On the other hand, what was left for her there?

What could not be named and described by my mother started only a few houses away. She was an intelligent woman who had been crushed in childhood by terrible poverty, about which she could not speak. What my father liked to talk of as the real world had for her no geography. She ate, she slept, she asked no questions of life for fear of getting a crushing answer. The Americans had crashed into this gloom like sunlight.

It has always baffled me why my parents did not divorce after the war, for my father had enough accumulated evidence of adultery to destroy her; and in some part of herself that was exactly what she wanted. She, too, was under forty: her sense of her own worth was at an all-time low. She had hardly seen him since 1940 and the arrangement he now made – to come home at weekends when it suited him – was to last until 1952. It was marriage converted to a prison sentence.

Though we lived like the poverty-stricken and benighted people my mother believed us to be, we were not by any stretch of the imagination poor, measured by the salary of the only breadwinner. My father was already better off than the neighbours I saw walking to work with their sandwiches and thermos flasks tucked into gas-mask satchels. He had developed a metropolitan taste for the best – silver cigarette lighters and super-thin cases, expensive shoes and carefully chosen suits. But what he earned and how he spent it was none of our business. My mother had in her an ineradicable fear that one day the material world would come crashing down about her ears and what little she had would be taken away. My father knew this could never happen but it was not in his nature to comfort or console. After all, moaning about life got you nowhere. Just look at his own triumphant progress: was there an ounce of self-pity in that? There was not.

His youngest brother, with whom he finally went to lodge, was the famous sand dancer. Jim lived in a flat on the Bartholomew Estate in Kentish Town with his wife Jessie and their children. On one side of the road, the early Victorian stucco villas were privately owned. On the other they belonged to the council. Divided, they made spacious and even elegant flats, more like New York apartments than the usual run of council property. The area was comfortingly smoky and louche but had connections with the leisured past that even the railways had not been able to obliterate.

If there was ever an idea of the perfect couple in my mind it was Jim and Jess, the steadiest and wisest members of the whole extended family. He was burly and buck-toothed, a man who laughed a lot, smoked, drank and acted the goat. Yet inside him was a lake of calm. The French would have recognised him at once. He was *un homme sérieux*. Jessie was tall and stringy and to my eye much resembled Katharine Hepburn. Her glamour was of a completely different order to my mother's — she was extremely beautiful without making the slightest effort. She wore slacks and black-and-white print blouses, had a father who played the violin and a brother-in-law who lived upstairs and seemed to me to spend his life waiting to be called down to entertain us with his snare drum and brushes.

Life had dealt these two high cards. They loved each other without having to think about it. Their special knack was to make time slow down, so that in their company there was always a feeling of unbuttoned relaxation. Everything was interesting to them, from the foibles of the close family to the fate of the world. On Thursdays Jim filled out his pools coupon without the faintest idea of what he would do if he was made rich. He was rich already. He had left-wing politics but never really expected the world to get better. He was a master mechanic who did not own a car, a sculptor in wood who never visited a gallery. He was in truth everything my father was not. He had sized the world to his own liking and found it endlessly fascinating.

Jessie was his perfect complement. Once, just before Christmas, I went to Bartholomew Road and found her standing on a chair with a child's paintbox, colouring the berries on the ancient acanthus wallpaper.

'But since we ain't got no steps, the festive season only goes halfway up the wall. So the top half is where the frost is cruel, see?'

When Jim came home that night, he washed the oil and grease from his hands at the sink and let the rabbit out for a run. Newspaper was spread on the table and we sat down to eat, the rabbit hopping from plate to plate. Covertly, I watched my cousin Michael to see if he knew how lucky he was.

'Your dad's late tonight,' Jessie observed to me.

'He's probably playing snooker up the Reform Club,' Jim murmured equably, rolling a cigarette and passing it to me to lick the paper. 'With his mates. Lord Portal, Anthony Eden and that lot.'

'Wasn't you asked?'

'I had to come home and talk to Michael's bloody rabbit, didn't I?'

In Cambridge, my mother attempted to make the best of a bad job. I would go out in the morning with the three-piece suite still in the front room and the dining table and chairs in the back. When I came home everything would be changed round, at the expense of ruined wallpaper and deep gouges in the plaster: she manhandled the bulkiest items with a giant's strength. This all-change happened about three times a month. The kitchen was repainted a thick buttery yellow from tins she bought from an ex-WD store at the bottom of Mill Road. It was probably surplus to the campaign in the Western Desert and designed for use on tanks and trucks. Huge reproachful stars lay stuck to the lino.

Together, we made an attack on windows that had not been cleaned for years. The ruined curtains were torn down and burned in the middle of Lord Muck's lawn. She no longer bought woollen sweaters at jumble sales but, to brighten the place up, pictures of hunting scenes framed in passe-partout and – above all – pretty well anything that could be polished. We became a home for discarded knick-knacks – brass bells, ashtrays, shell cases, horse brasses, Benares trays. There was hardly a surface in the ruined front room that did not display these things. Even the revolving bookcase became a repository for letter openers, brass inkwells, miniature cannon and every kind of bird and animal. The scent of Blue Moon that used to haunt the house was replaced by a different fragrance. The ground floor stank of Duraglit.

The centrepiece of my mother's enthusiasm was a plaque of a galleon in full sail which hung over the crowded mantelpiece.

'Lucky bastards,' she said of the invisible crew pounding along through the Spanish Main.

'I want you to leave the effing furniture exactly where it is,' my father bellowed on one of his pastoral visits. 'Is that clear? And if you are going to paint the kitchen, you *move* the cooker and the rest of the stuff, you don't just paint *round* it. Get him to help you,' he added, pointing to me.

'*Him!*' my mother cried incredulously. 'Old Tin-ribs?'

He retired in a huff to the front room, where he sat alone, smoking and conjuring affairs of state. Only a little while after rejoining civvy street he had been required to sign the Official Secrets Act, something as important to him as his Mention in Despatches. It seemed that the King, whose attention had first been drawn to Bert for his part in the Arnhem drop, now had further use for him – service of a kind he was not at liberty to divulge. Had we been the most lovingly discreet family in Christendom he would not have told us, but it must have been especially galling to come home from office meetings held in high secrecy to a shabby and underlit room where there winked and glinted enough brass ashtrays to furnish a pub. A cobra with one ruby eye missing had, on its blind side, a bird my mother believed to be a stork. He took them both and threw them into the garden. Next week they were back.

Some years later my father told me what his secrets were, using his own shorthand version of postwar history. By then I was a graduate but unlikely – in his eyes doubly unlikely – to have the faintest bloody idea of what was going on in the real world. We could agree, could we not, that the Germans were no longer the enemy? Bomber Harris had seen to that. Well, then, when Old Winnie was kicked out by an ungrateful public, the milksop nancy-boy Labourites who could not organise a piss-up in a brewery had put the country once again at risk. It was Ivan nowadays who was trying to make fools of us. It was not to be mentioned to another living soul, but in the event of nuclear war, Bert was part of the plan to spirit the Government underground, where the fight would continue come what may. There was a hole under Holborn that would make my eyes pop. Except, of course, it was none of my business.

As for my mother, huge mauve rings began to appear under her eyes and her neck became stringy. She was up to sixty cigarettes a day. Now we never opened the door to *anyone*, which led to ridiculous scenes with the gas man banging on the downstairs windows, his face distorted with rage, or the postman holding up occasional parcels and waggling them, like a zoo-keeper trying to entice particularly difficult animals out into the open. Anything posted through the door in a buff envelope went straight in the bin: when threat of legal action followed, she shoved the letter into her own buff envelope (she had bought a fire-damaged pack of five hundred at a jumble sale) and posted it to Lambeth Walk, without commentary.

'I know you are in there,' someone in a suit shouted through the letter-box one day.

'I am. And I know my rights. So you can sod off.'

Early one morning I went out to buy Peggy some cigarettes. When I came back she fished a crumpled piece of
paper from the shelf that held the saucepans and their lids.

'It says here that you've to go to that school at the top of
the hill this morning.'

'What for?'

'How do I know?'

I read the letter. It was a requirement for me to sit the
eleven-plus.

'What does it mean?' I asked, alarmed.

'If you don't go, you won't find out.'

I looked more carefully. Whatever it was, the examination
was taking place in twenty minutes.

By this time I had a bicycle, as did practically every
household in Cambridge. I cranked up Cherry Hinton Hill,
a route I was to get to know only too well in the future, often
filled with the same degree of blind panic. The school, now a
Sixth Form College, flourished then under the title 'The
Cambridge and County High School for Boys', as announced
on a dark blue board with faded gilt lettering. Milling about
in the playground I could see perhaps a hundred candidates,
some of them with pencil boxes, some even with satchels. I
rode in through the gates and had the handlebars seized by a
large man sporting a magnificent moustache.

'You don't *cycle*, not in *here*, laddie. This is not some car
park. We're not –'

'Is that boy sitting the exam?' called a voice from the doorway to a single-storey building. The man with the moustache looked at me.

'Well, are you?'

'I think so.'

'Then double away round the other side and leave that horrible thing in the sheds and double back here, pronto. And tuck your shirt in. Pull up them socks. Just got out bed, have you?'

I saw that I was talking to the caretaker and not the headmaster.

I sat the examination that morning in a daze. Though parts of the paper nonplussed me, I could see in the whole an invitation as beguiling as any I could have imagined. The people who devised this test were obviously wonderfully clever and devious people, of a kind I had never before met. The invigilating staff were probably clerks from the education offices, but I saw them as giants, albeit not in giant form. They wore stiff blue suits and starched collars and their shoes squeaked as they walked. There was power in their balding heads and finicky white hands, in the pens and pencils sprouting from their breast pockets. From time to time their chief drew out a silver hunter and snapped the lid open with a dry crack.

The school itself was as entrancing as, say, Balliol might be to any student walking through its gates for the first time.

The place where I had been stopped from cycling was even laid out a little like a quad with a rose garden in its middle. Where the tarmac left off was an enormous field, stretching all the way back to the railway lines. The light falling on its dewy grass gave it the appearance of a vast sugared pastry and as far as I could tell it had no purpose other than to be. There was not a sign of goalposts, nor even any hint that it received so much as a footfall. While I was staring at it, the caretaker walked past with a wheelbarrow piled high with chemical apparatus, as nonchalantly as if he had been transporting logs of firewood. He was whistling.

The place where I had left my bicycle was easier to read and understand. A smaller court was made there of crushed clinker, to one side of which stood wooden prefabricated sheds. Before I left, I peered through the window of one of these. Thirty desks were arranged in five silent rows. A small dais bore the teacher's desk, on which rested half a dozen dusty books. The blackboard was wiped clean except for a single smudged word: *equilateral.* Whatever it meant – and I had no idea – it was powerful ju-ju of some kind.

'That's what they're for, to teach you all that,' my mother explained. 'When do they want you to start?'

We both believed I had come home from sitting the entrance examination to this wonderful place. She herself had left school at twelve and what education she had got since had come from talking to other people. What they told her was filtered through an extra-fine mesh of suspicion and disbelief, but some of it trickled down. Her principal understanding of the world was that authority was out to get you – not just policemen and magistrates, but bank clerks, ticket inspectors on the rare train journeys she made, council officials and – for her, tragically – doctors. The way to survive was never to make a wave and, if possible, never to give up your real name. So it was unsurprising that she viewed the Cambridge and County High School as a form of threat.

'Wouldn't you be happier down the road?' she asked. She was indicating a nearby secondary modern school about which she knew little but which was recognisably a school in her own idiom. There, what she called scruffy herberts slugged it out with grey-faced teachers whose first duty was to prevent the place being burned down, or so she said.

'This one's better.'

'More la-di-dah, you mean.'

I consulted Gloria Wilkes, the girl who considered me common. She gave the grammar school the thumbs-up, since it was her uncle's old alma mater and Uncle Richard, as she called him, had gone on to be an assistant harbour-master in Dover. Gloria was aiming higher: she was going to be a doctor when she grew up. This seemed to me to be looking impossible distances into the future.

This conversation took place on a cycle ride to Cherry Hinton. At other times Gloria, accompanied by her father, had gone even further afield, to the Gog Magog Hills. They had taken a picnic to this wonderful place and the two

explorers had lit a fire and made tea, using an old kettle otherwise kept in the garden shed. I don't know what I hated more
– her ambition to be a doctor or the fact that her family
had two usable kettles. But the day was not over. After an
awkward silence while sitting against a chalky bank, the front
wheel of her bicycle spinning from my occasional kick, she
suddenly turned to me.

'I need to go to the lavatory. I shall climb through this
hedge and I don't want you to look. That has got to be clear.'

'What do I care?'

'Well, you should care. It's very important that you don't.
Look, I mean.'

She crawled through the hedge and walked off fifty yards
or more, disappearing behind a fold in the ground. When she
came back her wrist and forearm were pricked red by nettles.
But we had nettles in our garden and like the battlefield
surgeon I would never become, I found her a dock leaf to
calm the rash. She clutched it to her arm with a surprisingly
square hand and for an instant our skins touched. We sat
there blushing like fools and deafened by skylarks. I had
already noted Gloria's sturdy legs and plump arms. Now she
took her sandal off and brushed a little dust from her toes, a
thing she did with such absorption I was entranced.

'You can go too if you want.'

'Where?'

'Oh, don't be such a *nit*,' she said comfortably. She
smiled, showing lots of very healthy front teeth.

And after all, what was I to her but a bony and unlovely boy with faintly sour-smelling skin? Gloria read Arthur Ransome. On some evenings she sat with her father and listened to improving talks on the radio. In the privacy of her bedroom she tootled on the recorder before sleeping in pyjamas between clean and lavender-smelling sheets. Every window in the house she lived in was curtained and those curtains, she assured me, were lined. My mother knitted like someone sitting under the guillotine: Gloria's mother was a dab hand at the sewing machine, enough to line curtains and make her own dresses. There was a photograph album in Gloria's house showing the principal members of the family, their dogs and holidays, all the way back to the 1920s. Every postcard ever sent to Number 68 was kept in a shoebox, of which Gloria had been recently appointed custodian. Daddy sometimes made an awful stink in the lav. Mummy had Jack Hulbert's autograph.

I knew all these things because Gloria told me them. She too had sat the eleven-plus, though it gave her a blinding headache, almost exactly the same as she got from eating frozen ice-cream. She was looking forward to senior school, which came recommended by Miss Pybus, a friend of her mother's and a fellow worshipper at the Congregational Church. Miss Pybus taught French and German at the Cambridge and County High School for Girls, the existence of which came as complete news to me.

'Well, it's time you woke up,' Gloria said, wobbling back

up Cherry Hinton Road. 'See that dog there? It's a grey-hound. They eat nettles.'

The idea that my intelligence was being measured by the eleven-plus would have filled me with blind panic had I known about it at the time. It would have brought gouts of sarcasm from my mother: people like us did not have measurable intelligence. That was for other people. If she thought about my future at all, it was to bewail my lack of employable skills, in simple things such as replacing light bulbs, or painting and decorating. Once, when the flush on the lavatory gave up the ghost, the two of us stood on chairs peering into the cistern, baffled.

'I think I can fix it with a hairgrip,' I suggested dubiously.

'That sounds very bloody likely.'

But there was down the road an older boy, newly apprenticed to a garage. He fixed it, whistling, and then asked me back to his house for tea. His mother gave me a boiled egg, the first I had ever tasted. I knew what it was but not how to open it. She and her son exchanged glances.

'Show him your old motor-bike that you're mending, Charlie,' she said after we had eaten.

'It's all in bits at the present,' he explained as we stood under a canvas lean-to he had built. 'But I reckon I can get it to go.'

'Does your dad help you?'

'That wouldn't be half the fun, see? He *would*, if I asked him. But I don't want to.'

'How do you know where to start?'

He laughed uneasily.

'Bit obvious, that,' he said, gesturing to the cylinder block and what seemed to me a pile of unrelated metal.

He was pointing to the other path, the one I was destined never to take.

In 1947 I pitched up at the High School with a new pen, several stubs of pencil and a painfully yellow boxwood ruler measuring in inches and millimetres, all of which I held in my hand. My mother rose to the occasion with a new pair of shorts, some jumble-bought shoes and a black cap that was to be worn to and from school. This was our badge of rank and our means of identifying ourselves to the public at large. Nobody told us that first day it was permissible to take off the cap when inside the school grounds: we hung together like starlings, our black heads bobbing uneasily.

The school had a roll of six hundred that met for assembly in a 1930s hall of blond wood and polished floors. I found myself attending my first Christian service, with a reading from the head boy, prayers and lusty hymns. The staff was ranged on the school stage, all dressed in gowns, the headmaster at the centre. Various notices were given out, one of which was to welcome new boys. It was received in total silence.

We filed from assembly into one of the wooden huts, where we were greeted by the man who was to be our English teacher. Tall, faintly absent in expression, with gentle manners only occasionally ruffled by exasperation, Mr Hollingsworth called the roll and explained what was expected of us. Neatness of handwriting came top of the list, followed by punctuality in delivering homework. He scratched his neck and gazed out of the window for a moment or two.

'Working hard is enjoyable,' he said, addressing the remark to the mild sunshine that was making the windows of the assembly hall burn red. He yawned guiltily and turned back to us, polishing his glasses on a grubby handkerchief. 'I hope you can find it in you to do good work here,' he concluded.

A distant bell rang. Hollingsworth started, searched the pockets of his shapeless grey flannel suit and dragged out a piece of paper. He picked up chalk and stood in front of the blackboard for a moment or two and then began scribbling and slashing vigorously.

'Copy this down. It's your timetable.'

His handwriting was illegible.

The purpose of the great field at the back of the school became clear. At break, six hundred boys invaded it, whooping, chasing, playing football with ancient grey tennis balls, and very occasionally talking to one another in voices lower than a shout. We new boys hung back, not daring to stray far from the end wall of the assembly hall, some of us still holding timetables, some dutifully sporting their new caps. While I watched, a dispute broke out which led to wrestling and punching between two older boys. At once a crowd of about thirty was formed round them, jeering and chanting.

'Fuck that,' a country boy said reverently. He spoke for all of us. We huddled like sheep, driven this way and that for a few paces by a ball that flew our way, or as some laughing fool tried to escape capture by his friends.

'I thought this was a rugger school,' someone whispered.

'Got to be, the way these clowns play football,' a boy called Dillon said cheerfully. The next time a tennis ball came his way, he stunned it, flicked it up with the toe of his shoe and hit a low volley into the pack of sweating fourth-formers. He ignored their stares.

'If you want a fag you go down there, do you?' he said, indicating the railway lines.

'I smoke out in the barn at home,' a big slow farm boy said with a goofy smile.

'Was I talking to you, *Arth*-ur? I was talking to him,' Dillon said, pointing to me.

'My name's not Arthur.'

'I thought all you swedes was called Arthur.'

He was originally from Silver Street in north London and his father was a bookie. We exchanged a few comments about the Smoke and what to do in Cambridge when the police stopped you for riding a bicycle without lights, something that had never happened to me but seemed to be a regular thing with Dillon. His advice was to burst into tears and scream, 'Don't hit me.'

'Works every time,' he said.

'Was your dad in the war?'

He stared at me with a pitying half-smile on his face.

'He's a bit more clever 'n that,' he said gently, as a bell rang and we all trooped back to class.

One by one the staff announced itself as more than a set of names and subjects. Some teachers burst through the door, their gowns billowing, some sidled in with no more than a pained expression as their way of introducing themselves.

The man who taught maths was an Indian in the mould of Mr Banarjee. His teaching method was to raise questions that hung in the air like reproachful djinns.

'If we knew that a chestnut tree away in the distance was fifty feet high and if we had some way of measuring the angle from the horizontal at which we can see its topmost branches, what else could we find out?'

I was – of course – seeing chestnut trees, slit trenches dug to get down to ground level, conkers strewn about under the tree, dogs, almost anything. The boy next to me put up his hand.

'We could work out how far away the tree was,' he said calmly.

'Would you come out here and show us how, by sketching on the blackboard?'

This precocious child at once rose, his hand held out for the chalk.

I explained my misery over this little scene to my mother that night.

'Who cares?' she asked. 'Who cares about some silly bloody chestnut tree? And what's this?'

'Homework.'

'What, they expect you to carry all them books up and down every day? And what's *this*?'

'Latin.'

She was impressed, enough to give the textbook a wipe over with a damp cloth.

'Well, don't ask me to help you,' she said, unnecessarily.

All the same, while I was doing my first day's homework, which I did at the kitchen table with my brand-new plum-coloured fountain pen, she laid down at my elbow that rare treat, a cup of cocoa. Even more astonishingly she wafted the smoke from her cigarette away from my face, as if wishing to give me every possible advantage in the cogitation required to answer some pretty obvious questions.

'Take your time, Einstein,' she said slyly.

When I had finished, she studied the brand-new exercise books with real curiosity and read a page or two of the Latin primer.

It didn't last, this solicitude, but it was memorable.

'Of course,' Gloria said. 'You are always moving at the speed of the slowest. For now, anyway. I expect it will get harder and then the dopes will drop off, or be moved or something.'

'The *dopes?*'

She blushed. The girls' grammar school had given her more than one slang expression. She wore a grey skirt and green stockings, a tight green jumper and a white blouse. I was pleased to see that ink stained the joint of her second finger, taking it to be (at last) something less than perfect about her, though it may have been a carefully preserved sign of diligence. The other thing that interested me about Gloria, something I was hardly in a position to comment on, were the bumps that filled out her jumper. Dillon, whom I only ever saw at break, was a bit of an expert on the maturation of girls. He had a sister at Gloria's school. She was, as he put it, a big girl.

'Her!' Gloria squealed. 'She's *awful.*'

'So's her brother,' I said.

Most evenings we hung about between her house and mine in the hour between the end of school and dusk. We leaned on our handlebars like friends meeting intimately over an invisible table.

'What sort of marks do you get? Out of ten?'

'Eight, sometimes nine,' I said, omitting maths. Gloria was impressed enough to look irritated.

'Bet you don't.'

'Bet I do –'

'Don't.'

'How about you?'

'The same. Daddy's really pleased.'

'What's it got to do with Daddy?' I asked, with some of the rasp my mother would have given the question. Gloria straightened up at once and backed her bike away.

'You are *horrible*,' she said, cycling off into the misty evening.

That first year at secondary school was one of the great romantic adventures of my life. It is quite common for people who fall in love to find the material world transfigured, so that, for example, a particular bench in some city park will never seem the same again. It was like that. I was in love, not so much with the fabric of the school building but with the great body of knowledge that it housed. I had not known, for example, that the Romans had once conquered Britain, nor that their pots and coins were still being turned over by the plough, their roads still ran as straight as arrows. The French, whose language we had begun to mangle, had overthrown a king, only to raise up a tyrant who had in turn been bested by a man called Wellington. The battle at which he was dished was called Waterloo, 'a place-name some of you may recognise from your visits to London'. Indeed.

Egged on by Hollingsworth, I joined the branch library where I borrowed books from the children's section and furtively looked up *Gray's Anatomy* on the reference shelves for information about the parts of Gloria I had not seen nor was ever likely to see. The reading matter in the children's section was abysmal and I persuaded my mother to join the main library. Using her card, I borrowed the ludicrous novels of Rafael Sabatini and anything else that depicted panting bosoms. My father thought this kind of thing – reading books – effete. Walking down Mill Road on one of his weekend visits, he saw two pairs of scuffed boxing gloves in a junk shop, which he bought and brought home. We stood on the lawn while he toughened me up with a nose-bursting left jab or two. When I fell over, dazed, he laughed.

'A sight more useful than reading books. Now get up and defend yourself.'

On other occasions, he set me impossible herculean labours.

'Next time I come home, I want to see this garden dug over, front to back. And fix that trellis.'

'How?'

'How? Ask yourself, how would *I* fix it?'

'Except he's eleven,' my mother pointed out.

'You want him to grow up like a girl, do you?'

'Fix your own bloody trellis,' Peggy advised him, going into the house and slamming the back door with the noise of a rifle shot. My father tossed his cigarette into the weeds and began whistling, always a sign of contemptuous dismissal.

'When are you coming home for good, Dad?'

He broke off hissing through his teeth.

'Look, get this straight. I have work to do.'

'But everybody has work to do.'

'You think so, do you?'

I already understood about my father that he based his relationships with the world on the parts that were useful to him. So, anything to do with school appeared to him irrelevant. He did not bother to learn the names of my teachers any more than he would wish to memorise the Arsenal line-up. The stare he gave me now sent a shudder straight through me. I too was part of the furniture of the world he could safely discount.

There was a sudden huge crash and the sound of falling glass. My mother, who was way ahead of me in reading his character, had thrown the Clarice Cliff rabbit through a pane of the french windows behind us. Whistling again, Bert-turned-Tommy measured the aperture and sent me off to a builder's yard where by now we were quite well known. The glazier was also a whistling man, though his speciality was a warbling rendering, rich in tremolo. He was too old to have served in the war and wore a brown linen coat with an artificial rose pinned to the lapel.

'Nelson Eddy,' he explained.

I took him to mean that the glass was ready. He smiled and with the utmost casualness reached out and cupped his hand between my legs. It was, as I understood it, a friendly gesture, even an act of reinvigoration. He waggled his eyebrows.

'Try to get this home without breaking it. And in future tell your dad to fetch his own bloody glass.'

He walked away, whistling.

To spite my father, I told him this. The muscles in his jaw jumped and he examined his hands, flexing them as though to test how swiftly they could be made into fists.

'I ought to go back there and deck that bloke right now,' he said in a thick voice. 'The country's full of these jumped-up nobodies. Next time you see him, *you* tell *him* that I'm trying to make a man of you, give you some responsibility in life. I know what went on here in the war. I'm not stupid. You could have done more.'

I was flabbergasted.

'Like what?'

'You shouldn't have to ask,' he said.

Chapter Five

THERE WAS A PITCH DOWN A MUDDY LANE AT THE side of the grammar school where we were taught the elements of rugby football – how to kick and catch a ball, the right and the wrong way to tackle. These lessons, which took place in all weathers (even, one memorable December morning, in a Dickensian snowstorm), were conducted by a sardonic Mancunian who had already discovered his fleck of gold in the heap of spoil that was the first-year intake – the one natural ballplayer among us.

Mr Eckersley was as fit as a flea, though his glory days were in the past. He was clever enough not to reveal what those days were, so that some said he had played rugby for England while others insisted his real game was county cricket. The desire to elevate members of staff to the status of hero was common. Hollingsworth had written a thriller so heated it could only be bought under brown wraps; Mansell who taught Spanish, had captured Goering (whom he a little resembled) at the point of a service revolver; Perkins (maths) had spent the war as George VI's private detective. These fantasies proliferated. We were, it seemed, taught by men whose medals and testimonials had been hidden away in secret drawers. Or you could believe Dillon.

'They came out the war knackered and it was this or selling vacuum cleaners. Simple as that, cocker.'

Sightings of the staff in their private lives were gleefully reported. Howell had been spotted walking into the Blue Boar carrying a teddy bear under one arm; Mr Hollingsworth talking to a point-duty policeman, his bicycle round his ankles. The gifted and decent man who taught Latin was seen one foggy autumn evening kicking a dog in the street. Even the headmaster had a life outside the school. His MG was witnessed being winched out of a ditch on the road to Newmarket, the bonnet festooned with weeds. These reports were elaborated and passed from mouth to mouth in the playground.

There was a far more plausible explanation for the character of the staff. Though there were some who were too old to have fought in the war, the greater part of those who taught us had only recently thrown off uniform. The mystery that surrounded them came from the undoing of what they had been six years earlier. In this, we were a lucky generation of schoolchildren. Eckersley's sardonic manner, his hands-in-pockets insouciance, came from a more recent source than we imagined. Like my father, he had been lately exposed to a different world, one where the torpedo kick had proved to have less importance than the actual torpedo. He had come through.

The physically clumsy Hollingsworth had indeed published a crime novel but the state had found a way to employ his interest in murder that he had not bargained for as a younger man. The headmaster of such dashing looks left the RAF as a wing commander with the DFC ribbon on his chest. Putting it at the simplest level, we were being taught by men who had discovered that a liberal education at one of two universities was the least useful component of their wartime experience. They were busy picking up the threads of their profession in a much-changed world. A supply physics teacher called Mr Rogers led us through what was necessary to build a clandestine wireless receiver from basic materials.

'But you are using batteries, sir. How would you get hold of those?'

'You would bribe the guards,' he said calmly. Up until that moment I had been crouching in a wood with Armstrong's father, Sten gun close to hand, the plans of the submarine pen stuffed inside my shirt. I looked up. Mr Rogers had one hand laid over the palm of the other and was regarding his knuckles, caught in some private reverie.

'We will assume a suitable power source,' he amended.

But if he did not read Rockfist Rogan, we did. Moreover, we all had war stories of our own to tell. The war was a vast illustrated comic on which we lavished our attention and, since we had won, threw up nothing but heroes. That it had also caused a massive dislocation of feelings and attitudes was beyond me to understand, though there were local clues. In the assembly hall were honour boards, of the succession of headmasters, the captains of sport and even the principal house, going back to the 1920s, when somebody had thought such information worth memorialising. I can remember reading them and wondering about their awkward redundancy in the world as it was now.

I should have been more attentive. Though never stated, we were a collegium. Where we came from in the morning and what happened to us when the last bell rang in the afternoon was irrelevant. We were scholars, as much so as the languid young men sauntering through the gates of Trinity, or poling their girls in punts past the bathing station, gramophones keening. That a 1901 grammar school could work this magic with the materials at hand was a little piece of creative genius.

'What a joy!' Mr Hodges remarked, reading us part of Hazlitt on the Indian Jugglers one fog-filled morning when the lights burned butter-yellow and forty feet away the assembly hall took on the appearance of a passing ship. 'What a very great man he was, don't you think?'

He was talking to a sprinkling of boys from his own background but also to the sons of milkmen, train guards, farm labourers and petty clerks. His lessons were notorious for being off the point. Hodges, we all agreed, rambled. He was often hard to understand and returned our work with sardonic comments written in a minuscule hand while at the same time omitting to mark the essays out of twenty, as we supposed was his first duty. Some days he would come in and start a reflective monologue that only ended when the bell went. All these things made him a bad teacher in the purely technical sense and it may even have been that some colleagues looked at him askance. Yet what I know now about literature began in his amiable and discursive classes.

Mr Hodges was an historian.

Gloria was not sporty. It was Daddy's intention to teach her tennis when she was a little taller and, as she put it delicately, more agile. Hormones and school dinners were otherwise making her into a very solid presence, broad-shouldered, heavy in the beam and with a faintly suety glaze to her skin. Things had progressed to a dangerous state between us, as far as her inviting me into her father's shed when he and Mrs Wilkes were out shopping. I was shown the bird table he had built her when she was nothing but a baby in a pram, the kettle with which they made tea on the famous expedition to the Gog Magog Hills, and her grandfather's horticultural awards pinned to the cedar panels with drawing pins. Old Mr Wilkes had won first prize for his chrysanthemums in 1927.

'Where is he now?'

'Dead,' Gloria said vaguely. 'He fell out of a car.'

I looked at her closely.

'In Snowdonia,' she added.

121

I was about to ask her where that was when she suddenly plunged towards me, arms round my neck. Our teeth clashed. Her mouth tasted faintly of sour milk, her cheek of Nivea Cream. We wrestled about a bit, huffing and puffing. A spade clattered to the floor of the shed, followed by a cascade of ancient yellow newspapers. Young Mr Wilkes's shallots swung by their withered stalks over our heads. Gloria's father knew about horticulture, no doubt, but had he ever explained to her sexual arousal in the young male? It seemed not. What was poking her insistently on the hip and belly finally sent a message through to her brain. She looked at me for a moment, spit gathered in the corner of her mouth, her specs awry, before, sensible girl, she pushed me off and ran into the house, her school blouse hanging out at the back.

'Did you cop a feel?' Dillon asked at school on Monday.

'Yes,' I lied.

'I bet.'

'Her grandfather was killed falling out of a car. In Snowdonia.'

'That's nice,' Dillon said drily.

He was already drifting away to other and better company. There was a carelessness in him that seemed to startle both staff and boys. At break he had taken to playing football with fourth-formers, steaming into them with his head down. At the end of the day he cycled down Hills Road, hands in pockets, his cap on the back of his head, disgraceful blond curls wafting in the breeze. He was not Eckersley's fleck of gold, though he could have been. He played rugby with deliberate cackhandedness, saving himself (as he put it) for the weekend, when he turned out for a village football team against full-size yokels. His soubriquets there were worth having: he was variously dubbed the Eel, the Cisco Kid and Pocket Dynamite.

Gloria settled the confusion that had taken place under the shallots with a note: *Thank you for coming to see me on Saturday. I learned a lot about you. Yours sincerely, Gloria Wilkes.* As love notes go, it was not the most expressive and I took it to mean – correctly – *Keep your grubby hands off me.* The note was passed under conditions of great secrecy by another girl, with plaits and a goofy smile, the daughter of the greengrocer. She dropped the many times folded sheet of paper into a bag of potatoes, before collapsing into giggles. Gloria moved on to better things, cycling past our house with a blushing nod, or walking past hand in hand with Daddy on Sunday mornings.

'That gink,' my mother said, studying him from the window. 'I bet *his* life is worth living. And his kid's all bum. Look at her.'

True to his word, Mr Wilkes taught Gloria tennis that summer. I had adventures of a different kind with a boy from school my own age. We met in trembling secrecy wherever bushes grew in empty pasture, pulled down our shorts and masturbated each other like initiates of a solemn religious order. We rode out to the Roman Road, undressed completely, and ran up and down yahooing where once the tramp of legions had raised the dust. Kissing was out of the question, but wrestling was quite in order: in fact it was in its own way appropriate to the surroundings. The consequences were far more inflammatory than any kind of kissing I could imagine.

'The trouble is,' this boy said, his arm flung over my naked stomach as we lay panting in the dusty grass, 'we are super-brainy.'

'Sounds bad.'

'More than you think.'

'Except, I don't feel all that brainy.'

'You'll never fit in though,' he insisted. I sat up too suddenly and, good-hearted soul that he was, he flinched.

'We ought to stop this before it goes any further,' he said, holding me by one bare shoulder and brushing chalk and twigs from the small of my back.

'What does that mean?' I asked with a dry mouth.

'If you were a girl you'd know,' he muttered darkly.

Half a mile away was a huge stand of beeches. We cut our initials into a trunk we thought we might find again, using a penknife with a pearl handle, before cycling home in that way children have, nowadays the prelude to road traffic accidents but in those more innocent times the sign of friendship and affection. Pushing someone on to the verge, better still into a ditch, was mere cubbishness. But on this day of Roman wrestling, my mother, the Petulengro of romantic possibilities, took one look when I threw my bike down next to the dustbin and wandered in.

'You've been up to something,' she said.

At the end of the first year, I came second in class position. This was such an unlikely achievement that I pedalled down Cherry Hinton Hill like the wind and flourished the school report in Peggy's face.

'What's it to me?' she said. 'Nothing's changed here. We're still stuck in this rat-hole. What happened to your dibber?'

She was touching a very sore point.

The woodwork master was a sombre man struggling to keep us interested with no teaching materials to hand. For a whole year, he spun out his classes showing us how to make a half-joint from two raggy pieces of wood, something that might have taken a morning in a trade school. Instead we sanded, we measured, we remeasured, we oiled the tenon saws, we sharpened chisels, we boiled glue. It was in a way a masterpiece of teaching, to spin out for forty weeks the making of a potato dibber. A week before the end of the summer term I took mine home to present to my father, who happened to be there that weekend. I found him smoking in the garden.

'What's this?'

'A present.'

He turned it over in his hand once, twice, and threw it over the fence into Mr Blundell's garden.

'Get in the house,' he muttered.

My mother was right. We were not going anywhere. I already knew things they would never understand, not just about the subjects taught at school, for what did that matter? Slowly and haltingly, I was beginning to learn how to interpret the world from an educated point of view. Maybe they saw that, these two unhappy people. Each in their way would have assumed – in time did assume – that all this book-learning was being put in place to judge them.

There were boys in my class from homes that had pianos and book-lined studies; and boys who rose at five with their fathers, to help with milking before sitting on the icy churns waiting for the Cambridge bus to loom out of the mist. There were boys who were being taught musical instruments, or who went to the coast each summer on Pentecostal missions. There were boys whose fathers had been killed in the war. There was no boy who lived in the same road as me and none (or so I believed) whose parents hated each other with such venom as did Bert and Peggy.

A yawning gap opened between who I was at home and what the school expected of me. There, as Hollingsworth had been the first to point out, punctuality and working hard were everything. Getting homework in on time, changing classrooms swiftly (*walk*, don't run), remembering to bring the right kit to school mattered. As for working hard, though I was doing well, many of the lessons had as much relevance to me as, say, the study of Sanskrit. I simply repeated what I had been told with more or less accuracy. Job was afflicted with boils and scraped them off with potsherds. Double decomposition occurred when salts – I think this is right – changed places in solution. The beauty of a Shakespeare play was in its poetry, which was of a very high standard, remarkable (apparently) for a grammar school boy with little Latin and less Greek.

'And so what?' my mother demanded. 'They are teaching you all this so's they can earn their screw and then sod off for ten weeks of the summer. Leaving you mooching round here. What's it all *for*, that's what I want to know. That Alan kid down the road wants to be a baker when he grows up. What's more important, bread or Latin? Answer me that.'

I couldn't. The RAF had made my father a gentleman, according to his own lights. Grammar school was merely making me an inky swot. I knew this boy Alan who wanted to be a baker. He came from the secondary modern, where they played footie, smoked on their way home, and shared classes with sultry girls who wore their ties like necklaces. The lure of baking was not the only nor even the chief thing in Alan's life. What was beckoning him was not bread, but adulthood. Why else would he walk about with a moist black smudge under his nose, the beginnings of a man's moustache?

A more promising boy-turned-man came from a quiet house a few doors away. He wore corduroy trousers and a fair-isle pullover, often arriving by motor-bike to see his doting parents. He was a junior reporter on the *Cambridge Evening News*, a post that even the most cynical of neighbours accepted as a sign of having gone places. I was introduced to him by his father and when he learned I was at grammar school, he asked me what I was reading. I did not fully understand the question.

'Read Dos Passos,' he advised.

'Now there's a tip,' his father said proudly.

Long trousers made a difference. Stealing the occasional cigarette made another. Never mind Mr Eckersley and the laws of rugby: the way to stand against a wall was to have one leg crooked against it, the shoulders slouched, hands in pockets. Undergraduates walked through Cambridge with a stumbling head-forward action, as if about to trip over their glittering future. I preferred the backward-leaning American glide, perfected on the screen by the laconic Robert Mitchum who seemed pushed along in the small of his back by a troubled past. On a birthday visit to Lambeth Walk, I managed to persuade my father and an uncle to give me enough money to buy that brand-new thing, a pair of denim jeans. They were bought from a barrow on East Street market in Walworth. In Jockie's stock of useful screws and fixings, I found a handful of copper rivets that I hammered in at the corners to every pocket. With the legs turned up to make a huge white cuff, these jeans were a passport to a very different world.

'Ah! Modern times!' Mansell sneered as he barged past me one Saturday, books tucked under his armpit. It did not occur to me that he too was dressed for the weekend, playing the part of the donnish Thersites. He turned in at the Volunteer pub in Green Street, smoothing the wings of his hair, his yellow check jacket hanging on him like a horse blanket.

'And *this*,' Eckersley cried on another occasion, 'is – tell me your name again?'

I told him, watched by the girl he had with him, a heavy-featured and extremely bosomy blonde. She smiled encouragingly.

'Perhaps you'd like an ice-cream?' she suggested.

'Of course he wouldn't. Any more than he'd like an umbrella.'

At which she laughed, showing faintly mossy teeth.

This chance meeting took place in the gardens behind Drummer Street. Cambridge was notable for its green spaces: the famous areas like Parker's Piece and Jesus Common, as well as designated recreation grounds, where loose gangs of children would assemble in the summer evenings. I had the jeans, an ex-American sweatshirt and more often than not a handful of cigarettes stolen from my mother. My new mates were leery kids with acne, ink tattoos, and perspex rings made from B-17 cockpit windows. Any lengthy remark – almost anything longer than a grunt – was interrupted by farts. The intimate parts of the body were described in four-letter words that had long ago lost their novelty.

In my second year, 'going up the rec' became a fixed habit. We met up most evenings, though it soon became clear that our tribe was just one of several. In all our idle and aimless association, gobbing spit, farting, chatting up girls, there was always a lookout posted.

'Here comes Frankie!' was the signal for immediate dispersal, for the warning embraced not just Frankie but his gang, thundering towards us across the sodden grass, the cavalry on bikes from which the mudguards had been removed, the runners sometimes stripped to the waist, their narrow white chests gleaming in the dusk. Then it was a matter of heart-pounding flight, head down over the handlebars and pedalling for dear life. Frankie himself was a huge maggot of a boy with a steel brace on his leg. I lived in terror of meeting him alone, though of course alone he was bereft of all his powers.

The truth was that I hung out with these lads to pursue their sisters, wan and gum-chewing girls with bare legs and hunched shoulders, who could decide at a hundred yards whether a boy was worth encouraging. They moved in twos and threes and had no bicycles, nor the money for bus fares, but walked everywhere, the most precocious of them in their mothers' high-heel shoes. Some wore make-up, some slouched along as they had got out of bed that morning, unkempt and unwashed. Each had the power of a sorceress, drawing from the boys that flocked round them writhing snakes of lust. They were of course as unavailable as film stars.

Occasionally their older sisters would saunter past with their boyfriends on the way to a more remote location. These encounters were raucous.

'Eh, you! What d'you think you're on at, hanging round here with this load of monkeys? I'll tell Mum on you, see if I don't.'

'Ooh, is that *Clive*? Where'd you find *him*, in the dustbin?'

'You shut your gob.'

'You won't get nothing off *her*, Clive!'

As for Clive, so for me. By the conventions governing conversation in this setting, my speech was too muddy and far, far too allusive. Girls I did manage to snag looked at me with pity as I blathered on about American Forces Network or how their pubescent bodies were ninety-per-cent water.

'Then why don't we freeze solid like milk bottles, when it's cold?'

At this same hour, in the world as defined by the grammar school, boys would be at piano practice, or listening to something improving on the Home Service, teaching the dog to balance biscuits on his nose, or reading.

'Do you have a gramophone?' one such asked, a child who eventually became head boy.

'I'd lend you it if I did.'

'No. What I meant was, do you listen to music?'

Using my mother's way of interpreting life, I took this to mean: I know you don't have a gramophone and I was only trying to patronise you by asking. The Wrestler chastened me for thinking like this.

'Most people are lonely. You must have worked that out by now. Grown-ups, everybody.'

'Is Hollingsworth lonely?'

'Of course. He's probably desperate.'

'Lonely isn't unhappy.'

The Wrestler looked at me.

'Clever,' he said, jealously.

But then I knew he spent *his* evenings writing a novel. It was eight pages long and he hid it in an old suitcase for fear it might spontaneously ignite and destroy his parents' house.

'You stand a good chance of being beaten up by these new friends of yours.'

'They're not friends.'

'What are they, then?'

The Wrestler ate three meals a day, slept in ironed and aired pyjamas, cleaned his teeth regularly. He had a two-drawer desk in his room at which he did his homework, with a map of the world on the wall and a shelf of ancient box files containing clippings from newspapers and weekly journals like *Time and Tide*. Not all these useful references were scholarly – the boxes included line illustrations of women modelling corsets and photographs of starlets cut from film magazines. In an otherwise blameless life the Wrestler's father, one of hundreds of men who claimed to have bowled Bradman in the nets, also subscribed to *Men Only*. From this, the son had scissored pictures of naked young women poking about in reed beds or leaning morosely against solitary elms.

It was true that his secret life, like mine, was composed of highly explosive materials, but it was very unlikely that either of us would end up in prison. This seemed only too probable with some of the people with whom I was now hanging out. They thieved from garden sheds, made regular shoplifting expeditions to the city centre, habitually entered cinemas by the fire doors. I could see the justification in all this: soppy though I was, the world was set up to advantage me and people like me. It was a sort of victory for them to vandalise it or steal from it while they could. A lifetime of long-sufferingness lay ahead. The road to obedience started out in a gathering ground of beaten-down saplings and discarded chip papers, flicked dog-ends and aimless scuffles.

'Show us your tits,' someone shouted one night to a bloomingly confident young woman as the prewar Austin she was in came to a halt before a traffic light. The man who was driving her – probably her father – got out, walked over and with the flat of his hand knocked the boy who had said this to the pavement. He glanced at me in my fancy jeans, a Lucky smouldering in my fingers, with such a look of contempt that I cringed.

'Little twerps,' the girl shouted, laughing. She might as well have been addressing me in person. She was Gloria as she would be in ten years' time.

'Well,' the Wrestler commented, 'you were asking for it.'

133

*

I could not expect my mother to keep me up to the mark but I was confused by what seemed to me my father's lack of interest, without realising what an enormous control over his emotions he had exercised, not just in the present circumstances but since childhood. Since we never spoke or acted as a family, the weekends we spent together were purgatory. My father discovered a yard which sold American war surplus, from which he bought entrenching tools, musette bags, strange little flashlights and brown kapok-filled bedcovers.

'You both like the Yanks so much, you can keep yourselves warm with these,' he muttered, throwing them into the dining room.

That was it: that was the real cause of all our woes. We were collaborationists in the late war. When he was on this theme, my mother would walk out into the garden and sit at the very end, smoking. Her perch was the huge pile of chalk he had dug out in the days before he volunteered. If she had enough cigarettes, she would stay out there long after dark, whether it was raining or not. He would send me out to coax her in. It never succeeeded.

'She'll kill herself one day,' he said uneasily, watching the tip of her fag move in little arcs in the dark.

He caught the train back to London on Sundays, often walking out without saying a word. It was a relief to cycle up to the rec and hang round with people who seemed to me utterly transparent emotionally, like window glass. At sunset, when a uniformed gatekeeper came round to force us out into the roadway before locking the gates, we drifted away like leaves. Going home, I peered into front windows where things were being said and done, plans laid, issues decided. Until I reached my own house, I counted myself luckier. I was as irresponsible as the drizzle that fell or the breeze that plucked at my shirt. I had no purpose other than to be. Of the two models offered to me – my father's searing ambition, my mother's empty heart – hers was the more attractive. Sitting out in the garden half the night, struck blue with cold, seemed to have a heroic nihilism about it. It was frightening; but as a commentary on our general situation, poetic.

We spoke less and less. When I left for school she would be in bed and when I came home she would still be there. I fetched her cigarettes for her, left notes to say I needed money for bread or potatoes, ate alone and went to bed myself when the sheer tedium of staying awake overwhelmed me. In the morning I would cycle to school, putting on my cap at the last moment, half asleep.

As for the excursions to the rec, she never asked me where I was going. There was no curfew. She interpreted demands for money to go on school trips or to buy things like football boots and rugby shirts as having come from high authority, something too dangerous to tangle with. I asked her for money and she asked my father. He would peel off a pound note with the most complete negligence and resume reading the *Telegraph*, something the other men at work had taught him. She never asked anything of him for herself.

At the end of my second year, there was a school dance. We had some interest in this as junior boys, for it was our job, on the day it took place, to dust the floor of the assembly hall with french chalk, turning it from a safe environment for children to a skating-rink hazard. A five-piece band was hired, of elderly men in claret blazers, their thinning hair plastered down with Brylcreem. I explained to my mother how important an event this was. The staff were more or less obliged to turn up, bringing with them their wives or dance partners: when else would we get a chance to solve the mystery of Hollingsworth's marriage, or witness the lumbering chemistry master take to the floor, there (hopefully) to break his neck in attempting the quickstep? The mayor himself had accepted an invitation to attend.

'The mayor,' she said, with a knowing laugh.

'You could come.'

'Only if you poked my eyes out first.'

'I would like you to come,' I said.

On the night of the dance chairs were disposed round small tables, lit by candles in jam jars. The band was led by a slob of a man playing tenor saxophone and the musical book was comfortingly soporific. The pianist was at least my grandfather Jockie's age. The quicksteps were poorly supported but there was much pleasure in watching the staff rise en masse for the waltz and the foxtrot. This was the first school dance since the winter of 1940, as the headmaster explained in a short speech of welcome. There might be more glamorous events of this kind held in Cambridge nowadays (laughter) but none more enthusiastically if inexpertly supported (laughter and the beating of table-tops). He hoped he might be allowed to add that for Mr Wagstaff this was an especially important evening, being a first peacetime opportunity to demonstrate the arts of Terpsichore he had acquired, or so the Head understood, in the arms of fellow POWs in Stalag Luft 7 (cheers and prolonged stamping of feet).

As he spoke, the swing doors opened silently behind him and my mother slipped into the hall, her hair pinned up, wearing a button-through floral dress. On her feet were the famous Cuban cork sandals. With the genius of the deaf, she had caught the mood of the moment and was smiling demurely. As the headmaster finished with a command to the band to let rip, he glanced round, saw her standing there and walked towards her with both hands extended. He murmured something, smiling, and she nodded. They whisked on to the floor to a quickstep. As with knitting, so with dancing: my mother was an untutored expert. So scintillating was their progress that it turned into an exhibition. Nobody else dared take the floor.

'Bloody hell,' the Wrestler whispered hungrily. 'Who is *that*?'

At the end of the music, they were applauded. My mother walked towards me with a curious expression in her eyes. She ruffled the Wrestler's hair and asked him to fetch her a lemon-ade. Sitting in the chair he vacated, she lit a cigarette and blew the smoke up towards the high ceiling.

'What d'you think about that, then?' she asked.

When I could find no words, she laughed and took my hand briefly in hers.

'Whoever that bloke is, he knows how to dance.'

'He's the headmaster.'

'Yeah?'

At last I understood the look in her eyes. For three minutes of not very good dance music, she had been the woman she had dreamed of becoming when a child in Lambeth.

Chapter Six

MY BROTHER MUST WONDER WHERE HE COMES INTO the story. He was born a serene and blond baby in the following year and for a time the balance of things altered for the better. He was extraordinarily good-looking, the sort of child that has strangers peering into the pram. My father thought of him as a superior model too, one to replace the botched essay that was myself. At weekends, he walked this more favoured son for miles, coming home with the canopy of the second-hand bassinet strewn with wild flowers and, in their season, conkers. He dictated what the child should wear and in what colours.

Something interesting happened with the redecoration of the third bedroom. My father approached the job with the same bullish enthusiasm that he gave to all trades that were not his own – in later life he laid bricks and built walls, replaced windows and rewired an entire house. Yet when he finished Neil's bedroom a strange fact emerged. He was almost completely colour-blind. Now we had a room in the house where one wall was red and three were green. The door was blue and the skirting boards grey. My mother and I inspected the finished result in awed silence. It was the first example of some terrible colour combinations he inflicted on us as the years went by but it was the cause that made the story.

Colour blindness to this degree would have prevented him from serving as aircrew under normal circumstances – the test was an essential part of the general screening programme and many before him had failed it. The degree of finish he had applied to the work in Neil's new bedroom was impeccable but there was something wrong and his face gave the game away. He had bribed the corporal in charge of his RAF test. It had cost him a pound note and forty cigarettes to get through to Air Training School.

'It was important for you to get in,' I suggested nervously.

'What do you think?'

Neil will understand me when I say that his arrival gives an astonishing twist to the story. Of all the things that might have happened to this shipwrecked couple, having a second child was the least likely. Some of those who stopped my mother in the street to exclaim about the new baby were as surprised to see her out of doors as they were to greet my golden brother. Twelve years separated her sons and what my mother had been in 1935 was by now much altered. The neighbours were cautious but I think also (many of them) delighted. In their simple way of looking at things, another child was just what the doctor ordered and better than any tonic.

She nursed Neil through his first months with unfussy calm. My father, when he was home, watched her like a hawk for errors and omissions but he was wasting his time. The house perked up. Until Neil's arrival we had no hoover and seldom if ever washed the lino-covered parts of the house. Now, what he could not clean by learning to crawl, we augmented with what my mother called 'a spruce-up', a weekly attack on dirt and dust. Many of the brass ornaments went into boxes under the stairs. The bell inscribed *Noli me tangere* was shown the dustbin after the baby ignored the warning and hit himself in the face with the rim.

At weekends, as I have described, my father threw himself into showing his son a good time. At bath-time, he sat on the floor, throwing soapsuds at Neil and squirting him with a water pistol.

'It can't last,' my mother said. 'He was like this with you.'

If he was, it was beyond my powers to remember. But she was right: little by little his interest waned. I realise now that what he was looking for in this guileless and good-natured child were signs of superhuman ability. Maybe he had done that once with me. As soon as Neil could sit up straight, he wanted him to crawl. When he could do that, he wanted him to walk. Most of all, he wanted his son to talk, to answer questions and reason for himself. He bought a bike and built a baby seat for it, one that was bolted to the crossbar and fitted with horse stirrups. Coming into Cambridge by train one Saturday, he noticed some linesmen laying track with the help of a crane. When he got home, he plucked Neil out of the garden and set off by bike to show his new son something he could learn from. They pedalled away with Neil yelling his head off in rage.

My mother was far more realistic. She built tents for the baby with the clothes-horse, made tubby potato men held together with matchsticks and, with the front door on the latch, stood outside and shouted peekaboo through the letter-box, a game that reduced my brother to a jelly. She baked gingerbread men with wild Afghan eyes made from currants and at mealtimes laid out peas on the kitchen table in the shape of a house or a fish.

But then, little by little, the old misery seeped back. What the doctor ordered turned out to be quack medicine: it could not save her. Now, when the Saturday quarrels began, Neil and I retreated to my room, playing gloomily and trying to ignore the bumps and crashes that were Peggy in full flow. On one occasion, Bert arrived by lunchtime and left again on the early-evening train. My mother sat in the ruins of the kitchen, glass and broken crockery on the floor, a huge mouse under her eye. Spit was gathered at the corner of her mouth and she looked utterly mad.

'I'm going to put my head in this gas oven tonight, you see if I don't,' she said.

'Don't do it, Mum,' I begged. I was holding Neil in my

arms. This was the room in the house where in the past we had sat gabbing over the table like two conspirators. Peggy rolled her head like a fighter trying to clear his vision.

'Your father is an ignorant no-nothing basket,' she said. 'Clear all this up and give Neil his tea.'

She pushed past me and swayed down the hallway. At the foot of the stairs, she turned.

'Don't ever ask me for nothing, Brian, because I haven't got it to give. Not to you nor no one.'

I sat up until one in the morning, guarding the cooker. Not the next day, but the day after, when she knew I had to go to school, she got up. Neil was sitting in his high-chair, eating a rusk and slurping luke-warm tea from a feeder cup. Peggy looked at me, one of her eyes completely closed. We seldom touched and hardly ever kissed but I put my lips to her cheek, trembling.

When Neil was coming up to two years old we went on our first ever family holiday to a boarding house in Hastings. Thinking about it now, the biographer in me is instantly alerted. The nearest coastal resort was Clacton, where most of the people I knew at school had been at least once. It could be reached by coach in a few hours and was notoriously chummy and easy-going. Hastings, by contrast, was two separate train journeys away and my mother, who I do not think had ever been on holiday in her life, was left to organise a major expedition. We packed as for an extensive beach holiday, filling a cardboard suitcase got from a jumble sale and a sailor's white duffle bag. The plan was that we would drag this kit to London, where my father would meet us and get us on the line to Sussex. He arrived at Liverpool Street wearing an open-necked shirt, his pipe jutting and a copy of the *Telegraph* under his arm. In his free hand he carried a brown paper carrier bag. It contained his shaving kit and a pair of ridiculous knee-length khaki shorts.

In retrospect, the choice of venue my father made seems a demonstration of his essential chippiness. He had not the faintest interest in Hastings as an historical site, though one of the photographs in Jockie's bureau showed the pugnacious bantam staring from the back of a charabanc in Battle. In that picture, my father was just a face peering over the side: maybe the memory spurred him on now, or maybe someone at work – and it would have been a superior – had mentioned the town with favour. The previous summer he astonished me by asking if I would like to go swimming. It was a trick question: we cycled sixteen miles to a hotel pool in Royston and then home again, a journey of over five hours. I was twelve years old (and could not actually swim). Like the marathon pram-pushing with Neil, this holiday was going to be an expression of doing things the right way – his way, the bulldog way. Not one of us, nor two of us, but all three of us were to be put on parade.

It was raining in Hastings and for all I knew had never done anything else. The boarding house was mean and crabby, with a handwritten list of RULES behind every bedroom door. There was to be no singing or dancing, no visitors after nine at night, all visitors to leave by ten. No primus stoves, no 'dogs or other animals', no wines or spirits to be consumed in the bedrooms. All these prohibitions were repeated verbally the afternoon we arrived by an unsmiling Mrs Parfitt, whose livelihood was got by treating her guests as the dirt under her feet. My father tried to interrupt her in his official voice: she simply stared him down. There was a Mr Parfitt, who had served in the navy, a great slug of a man who did the cooking. He was slightly more approachable but the tattoos on his forearms were a false lead. He had served out the war in a shore establishment.

'I was RAF aircrew,' my father explained.

'You don't say?' Mr Parfitt muttered, wiping his hands on his apron before retreating to the kitchen.

'We're going to stay in this hellhole, are we?' my mother asked.

The two things I remember most about the short time we did stay were going a little way down the coast to St Leonard's, where miniature cars and buses could be hired and driven about the seafront in sheets of water; and my mother's explosive reaction to being cooped up in one room of a strange house. Bert, having thought of the holiday, was ready to tough it out: she was having none of it. Mrs Parfitt, who thought she knew how to handle most human situations, was baffled. I listened to their conversation from behind the breakfast-room door.

'What don't she like about us?' she asked.

'Nothing for you to be worried about,' Bert said, in his official voice.

'Worried? I ain't *worried*! Any more yelling all hours of the night and you can sling your hook. That's how worried I am.'

We lasted two nights. There was no chalk heap on which to wait the time out and instead my mother sat on the un-opened suitcase. On the second evening, not to be beaten, Bert went for a saunter wearing his shorts. It was hardly nine at night, the brief but magic hour. My brother slept, his thumb in his mouth. I sat on the camp bed provided for me, shaking with fright. It seemed certain that at some point my mother would jump through the rotted sash window and crash to the dustbins and litter below. Inside the house, there was the steady patter of children's sandals running up and downstairs and the flushing of toilets. Further afield, the faintly frantic thrash of arcade music. Tested furtively on the tongue, my forearms tasted salty. We had yet to step on to the beach and now we never would.

That afternoon, in pelting rain, my father had taken me to inspect a small museum set up by fishermen on the quay. The exhibits were billed as 'denizens of the deep' and it was clear from the reactions of the other visitors that they were intended to amuse by their hideousness. Some were displayed alive behind glass. My father's cigarette smoke licked the walls of the tank as he studied them. Nothing dredged from the

English Channel can be so terrible as to frighten someone in balance with the world but I felt a deep shuddering revulsion in that sweaty cabin, the memory of which has never left me. All that was bad about us was metaphorised by those gaping mouths and bulging empty eyes: I felt myself go hot and cold and clung to the trestles on which the show was laid out. A huge meaty hand landed on my shoulder and a fisherman caught me before I fell. I was dragged out and dumped on to a box, where I sat with my head in my hands.

'Frightened of a few fish?' Bert scoffed when he came outside.

'Don't *you* ever get frightened?'

He was carrying Neil in his arms and hefted him to a more comfortable perch. The rain slashed our faces.

'Don't screech,' he said.

'You don't, then?'

He wiped the rain from his eyes.

'You're a weakling,' he said with his hissing mirthless chuckle. 'Like your mother.'

Now, I thought, *now* was the time to turn and run, pound down the black and silver sheets of the seafront pavement and cut up into the back of the town and so to the open country. Useless to make my way to Queenie, for she would only return me, but there must be somewhere and someone who would take me in. I suddenly thought of the Wrestler in pin-sharp detail: he was opening the door and ushering me to his room, there to embrace and undress me before laying out a selection of his clothes and pressing on me a wad of pound notes and a map of Paris.

'We'll go in there,' my father decided instead, indicating an amusement arcade. He jiggled his other, better son on his brawny forearm. 'This kid could do with an ice-cream.'

That night my mother sat by the open window, mute as stone.

'You're all going home in the morning,' Bert said to her silhouette. 'That's what you want, isn't it? You'll be happy then, you mad cow.'

The tide was full and the sound of waves crashing over the roadway lulled me to sleep. Next day, he left us in London to find our own way to Liverpool Street and the Cambridge train. It happened that every seat was taken and we stood in the whirling dust of the corridor, buffeted by passing strangers and the bouncing air that came at every bridge and cutting. My mother had not eaten or spoken for three days. She leaned her cheek against the shuddering glass, her eyelids flickering. The holiday had brought us to the heart of the matter, of what was wrong with us, we two wartime collaborators. We had been found wanting in gratitude. Nothing could drag us back to the ordinary concerns that animated our fellow passengers.

A well-dressed man in his fifties came out from a compartment and spoke a few low words to my mother. She was persuaded to take his seat, Neil on her knees. I studied her through the glass partition. Her head lolled.

'Have you come far?' the Good Samaritan asked me.

'From Paris.'

'Lucky chap. And what did you like most about it?'

'The Eiffel Tower.'

'Mmm. And the food? How did you get on with the food?'

'It wasn't anything special,' I said, making him laugh.

'Well, your mother is very tired. Will Daddy be meeting you at the station?'

'He was killed in the war,' I found myself saying.

The man patted my shoulder and lit a Gold Flake.

As if in mockery, the weather in Cambridge for the rest of that summer was warm and sunny. I took my bicycle to pieces and reassembled it, hung out at the swimming sheds on the Cam and at the open-air pool on Jesus Green, went to the cinema three times a week with money got from delivering papers. To my great mortification, Gloria, now lost to me for ever, had grown taller and slimmer and cycled past the house these days at breakneck speed. Once upon a time she had looked reproachfully into our front windows but now we did not merit a glance.

Neither my mother nor father had friends, or even in any social sense neighbours. Up and down the road other people did things communally, like sharing garden tools, cooking meals for the sick, or throwing birthday parties for their children. Old people had their gardens dug for them, young people fell in love. It was all very sketchy but it was a form of belonging. For most people, there was pride in living where they did. On summer evenings men mowed their front lawns and then, as an extra flourish, cut the verges that belonged to the council. The family that had flown the Brazilian flag on VE night bought a car and most Sundays it attracted a small knot of the curious who came to watch the owner effect minor repairs. We took no part in any of these things.

'If you think he's so wonderful,' my mother said after I described being asked by this neighbour to play in a charity cricket match, 'go and live there.'

Our house retained its blank, unwelcoming expression and was as difficult to enter as ever. My way in was to climb over a high fence in which was a gate that was nailed shut on the inside. A year or so of doing this had scuffed the creosote back to blond wood. Grass grew between the paving stones, the front gate hung on rusting hinges. It was the sort of property that normally belongs to very old people too poor to make repairs and too ill to do the garden.

The bike I had so studiously renovated and repainted took me no further than places I already knew. I went to the swimming pool alone and sat on the grass hugging my knees in shame for not being able to swim; at the cinema I was a mere spectator of other people's heroism.

'You made such a promising start,' Hollingsworth said of my schoolwork one misty November morning. 'I wonder what went wrong?'

'Dunno, sir.'

'What do your parents say about it?'

When I did not reply but squirmed like a worm on the hook, he nodded.

'I see. Well, it's a waste, you know.'

'It's alright for you to say that –'

Hollingsworth raised his long bony hands and put them over his ears.

'No, no, no. You really must see this as a job – and not a specially difficult one. The question is, will you botch it?'

'You asked me about my parents –'

'Oh, do let's leave them out of it. Parents are parents. You didn't choose yours, after all, any more than I chose mine.'

He frowned at me, a decent man who had gone one step too far and tumbled into banality. We were having this conversation at the conclusion of a particularly irksome lesson, with every inkpot filled with chalk and paper pellets bouncing off the blackboard. Hollingsworth very seldom lost his temper and never employed sarcasm. Wholeheartedness was his watchword and what he most often used as a weapon against us was genuine disappointment. When the bell rang, I had been surprised to be called back by name.

'Have you thought at all of what you might want to do, after leaving school?'

'No, sir.'

'You've never thought of it at all?'

'No.'

151

'Might you want to go to university, for example?'

I stared at him as if he were mad.

'Well?'

'I wouldn't mind being an actor.'

'Do you go to the theatre often?'

'A film actor.'

He frowned, jiggled his glasses higher on to his nose and glanced at his watch.

'Nothing is impossible,' he said generously. 'But unless you buck up, you'll go to the Remove next year.'

That lunchtime, a boy in the mould of Armstrong began pushing me round outside the huts. It was, to begin with, a quarrel about a tennis ball I had kicked over the straggly hedge, across the lane that led to the rugby ground and into some gardens. The boy was called Taylor.

'You skinny poof,' he said. 'You're useless, d'you know that?'

I was being pushed back by double-handed blows to the shoulders and chest. Taylor was counting on his height and weight, but unfortunately he was dealing with a boy who had just had it explained that one does not choose one's parents. Mr Hollingsworth had no doubt intended me to take this in a philosophical light but the remark filled me only with a sense of the rank injustice in the world. Taylor had chosen the wrong target. I closed my fist and hit him flush on the nose. We fell to the ground together and began rolling about, arms and legs flailing. A crowd formed immediately.

'Whose blood is this on your shirt?' the Head asked.

'His. Some of it's mine.'

'You also attempted to hit Mr Wagstaff when he came to separate you.'

'It was none of his business, sir.'

'So you thought you'd hit him, too?'

'I was out of control.'

'Evidently.'

The headmaster selected a cigarette from a silver case and regretfully thought better of it. Instead, he threw his feet up on to the opened lower drawer to his desk.

'It's a very boring story,' he said.

'Sorry, sir.'

He took out his pen and scribbled briefly.

'I want you to go home. Give this note to your father. Mr and Mrs Taylor will no doubt come down on you like a ton of bricks. Ready for that, are you?'

'He started it.'

'Oh *please*,' the Head said. 'Let me give you a word of advice. Make this your last fight, in school or hereafter. You will never be so lucky again. Would you say you need to be whacked by me, now?'

'Yessir.'

'You don't think that, so don't say it. Go home. Tell your mother you have been suspended for the afternoon for a brutal attack on a helpless sack of lard two years older than you. Shame on you.'

'He called me a poof.'

'Good God!' the headmaster suddenly bellowed, making me jump half out of my skin. 'Do you really think I have time to listen to all this? Get out!'

Taylor was waiting to go in and as I passed him in the office he very satisfyingly flinched, causing the headmaster's secretary to smile her wintry smile.

Taylor senior called at our house that evening. My mother was more than ready for him.

'Mrs T?' he asked jocosely, taking the wind out of her sails. There was a fashion among middle-aged men for zip-up golf jackets and he was wearing one.

'Your lad battered my lad at school today,' he said helpfully. 'I'm Cyril Taylor.'

'So?'

'Well, can I come in a minute?'

'No, you can't,' my mother said, adding, 'I'm busy.'

'Okey-dokey. I just came round to say he was asking for it.'

He held out his hand.

'What's this?' Peggy demanded, suspicious.

'Shake hands, no hard feelings,' Mr Taylor suggested.

He was quite clearly drunk. My mother shook his hand. He tried to peer round the door.

'Can I have a word with the kid?'

'He's too upset.'

'Oh ar? Well, just thought I'd pop round.'

'You've done that, then,' my mother said, closing the door on him in slow motion. I was hiding on the first tread of the stairs. She fluffed up her hair with both hands.

'Well,' she said. 'Fancy that.'

The note the headmaster had written in his beautifully elegant hand was on the kitchen table, torn into strips to make spills for the gas. She took a piece up and used it to light a cigarette. Beating the system, as she supposed I had done, gave her a warm feeling and she nodded to the packet.

'Help yourself,' she said. 'I know you do.'

It was a day of miracles. I refused the cigarette with as much indignation as I could muster and instead we sat down at the kitchen table for a chinwag.

'Now why does he call you a poof, this kid?'

'It was just something he said.'

'You're not, are you? You see a few girls, I take it. When you go out in your Roy Rogers outfit.'

'Jeans.'

'I daresay there's slap and tickle, though. That girl in the greengrocer's – she gives you the eye, I notice.'

'News to me.'

'What, a bit too skinny, is she?'

'Oh, *Mum.*'

'Just asking. So tell me this. Why do you put that Nivea on your face?'

I blushed crimson. 'To stop the spots.'

'But you haven't got any,' she said. 'And another thing. Who is Sonia?'

She held out an exercise book on which the name was written in elaborate drop shadow.

Sonia was a beefy backstreet girl with lank black hair. We met only occasionally though I often cycled round her neighbourhood hoping for a glimpse of her. When we did get together it was at the back of her father's shed on some sorry allotments. There she would stand stock-still, chewing gum, while I stroked her hair and kissed her neck. At the first sign that I intended to unbutton her blouse, her hand would come up and knock mine away. Otherwise, she was laconic in the extreme. It intrigued her that I was from the grammar school, as remote from her world as Jupiter or Mars. She was fourteen, the youngest of five sisters.

'Drives me dad barmy,' she said. 'More'n he already is.'

'What about your mum?'

'She don't say.' She thought about it a bit, chomping on her gum. 'She's fat.'

'What's that got to do with it?'

'I mean really fat.'

My erotic fumblings amused her.

'You know I already got a boyfriend, don't you?'

'You keep telling me.'

'Well, I have. You ent going to get nowhere. So why'd you do it?'

'Dunno.'

She took the gum from her mouth and squashed it on to a plank in her father's shed.

'Go on, then.'

'Go on what?'

'Just this once. Then I don't want to see you no more. Never.'

She pulled her blouse out, reached behind her back and undid her bra.

'Don't get all grabby,' she warned.

We kissed, while in the background dogs barked and the bus from town crashed gears. The way she stroked my hair was taken straight from the movies, just as the way I embraced her was less an expression of myself than of some other person, someone more apt for the moment. All the same, a great window soared open, disclosing a world I had so often imagined but never in such honey colours. Sonia laughed indulgently.

'You're a daftie,' she murmured, pushing me away. She did her bra up and buttoned her blouse. 'That's all you're getting. I told you, didn't I?'

We picked our way back to the road across glistening cabbages as big as footballs. My bike lay against a broken-down fence and as I picked it up a church clock sounded nine. It was the hour of curfew. Sonia studied me for a moment longer and then turned and ran towards the gas lamps, her heels clacking. I cycled home along the pavements.

I was delirious and awed in about equal measure.

Girls like Sonia were opening their blouses all over Cambridge every night of the week and it meant – among the sort of children who ran home to be in by nine – no more than a hurried adventure, or the exercise of a small but pleasing power. But in my own mind, then and for ever, it gave the idea of intimacy a name and a place.

'She wanted you to shag her,' Dillon explained.

'She's not like that.'

'What, she takes you out behind her dad's shed?'

'She's already going out with someone.'

'Yeah,' Dillon said, unimpressed.

But in fact I saw her with her boyfriend less than a week later. He was a tall and bony youth with a glowering expression. Hands in pockets, he walked towards me with Sonia half a step behind, his hair swept back in one massive black and glistening wing, spots caught in the crease of his scowl. He had no idea who I was, and Sonia passed me without a glance.

In the following year, I was put into the Remove. Those two high-fliers, Gloria and the Wrestler, became dots in the sky and I was down among the country boys, the willing but obtuse and the not-so-willing-at-all. The pace of lessons slackened, there was a great deal more insolence and clowning about. Homework became a chore, punctuality a comparative novelty. From being a willing boy I began to seek out trouble.

'A minor ability to imitate Danny Kaye isn't enough in life, I'm afraid.'

'Very funny man, sir.'

'Oh yes, *gifted.* Detention tonight, however.'

To my great surprise, I found an aptitude for playing rugby, enough to play for the school against a small league of similar institutions, but including the fearsome Bedford Modern, to which we travelled singing 'The Four and Twenty Virgins' and returned battered, bruised and silent. Second XV results were greeted at Monday morning assembly with more than usually sarcastic cheers. Although the backs were willowy enough, among the forwards were some of the biggest – and slowest – thugs in the school. I can remember at one away match the game being halted and the whole XV being given a screaming lecture on the offside rules by the referee, his mouth frothing with spit.

In the Remove, we set fire to the physics lab, intending only to create a small blaze by filling with methylated spirits the runnels that prevented pens and pencils from rolling off the benches. It was nearing Christmas and the idea was to introduce a festive note to the end of term. But things got out of hand. In the next term misrule spread to biology. We were taught this by a respectable young woman graduate in her probationary year. We nicknamed her Voodoo Lil. Her classes were specially chaotic affairs. In the middle of one, I was sent to the Head a second time.

'You have apparently been making a beast of yourself again.'

'Yessir.'

'It is alleged you put your hand between Miss X's legs while she was attending to someone in the row in front.'

'I was holding a ruler.'

'Yes or no?'

'Yes.'

'And?'

'It was done as a dare.'

'Was it really? The normal thing is to say that the punishment now coming your way is going to hurt me more than it does you. But I don't think so. Six on the backside. Bend over my desk, if you will.'

While I waited, I could see in front of me all the silverware the school awarded, ranged along the Head's mantelpiece. The pain of seeing these cups and shields from such a viewpoint was more humiliating to me than the swish of the cane. After it was over, I was directed to go to the staffroom and seek out Voodoo Lil to make my apology.

'You deserved what you got,' she said, uncertainly. 'It was a really stupid thing to do. Stupid, yes. And disgusting.'

'I'm really sorry, Miss.'

Being told by a woman that I was disgusting was more painful to me than being beaten. Unexpected tears welled in my eyes. When she stuck out a moist hand for me to shake, I seized it in gratitude. But the tears disgusted her even more and she snatched her hand back.

'Go away,' she said, curtly.

*

The man who most clearly represented high culture at school was the music teacher. We met once a week to watch him listening to gramophone recordings. With all the other teachers, their love of their subject could be excused as harmless enthusiasm. For example, listening to Howell ramble through the beauties of *Sohrab and Rustum* might have been thought pitiable among only slightly better educated boys, yet we indulged him out of admiration for his portly calm, which was that of a very superior royal servant. He came to his classes in perfectly cut blazer and flannels, decorated by a handkerchief tucked into the sleeve and a wine-stained college tie. By so dressing, he paid us a compliment. We knew very well that, given a choice, he would not have employed any one of us to shine his shoes. On the other hand, his love of the Victorian poetry he had learned himself when a child was touching, and sincere.

'Well, if it makes him happy,' someone said at the end of another excruciatingly dull lesson. Howell heard this and paused at the door.

'The intention was to make us all happy,' he murmured, without reproach.

By comparison, it was not as clear that the music lesson's purposes was pleasure. There were boys – a very few – for whom the recordings raised smiles of recognition. They sat at the front. The rest of us dozed or played a popular pencil-and-paper cricket game while letting the sound wash over us.

The man who taught us – and his grovelling acolytes in the front row – made no secret that what was happening here was akin to pearls being cast before swine. That was, perhaps, the whole point of classical music – that it raised itself above and beyond the coarser elements in life. It needed no explication. In any case, it was outside the remit of this idle and effete man to make music interesting.

That role was filled at school by the boy who played cornet, later on trumpet. The music *he* played came with an appealing history. Red-haired, even-tempered, with a wry sense of humour, David blasted out what used to be called traditional jazz, a catch-all title for music of the Mississippi Delta and New Orleans all the way up to Chicago. In 1935, the year of my birth, at a dismally received dance in the Palomor Ballroom in Los Angeles, the drummer Gene Krupa is said to have shouted to his bandleader, 'If we're gonna die, let's die playing our own thing!' That night, before a nation-wide radio audience, Benny Goodman, it is said, inaugurated the swing era.

The trumpeter on that broadcast was Bunny Berigan. Three years earlier, in the year of my parents' marriage, Berigan, the Dorsey brothers and two of the three Boswell sisters, went into a New York studio with a rhythm section and recorded 'Me Minus You'. Clearly, the event – and the sentiment of the lyrics – passed my parents by.

Me

Minus you

Means nuttin' at all;

But me

Plus you

Equals love.

Connie Boswell, who sang this number, was a childhood polio victim who spent most of her life in a wheelchair. She was born in New Orleans and this particular recording has always remained in my mind as the epitome of one kind of American music – effortless musicality that tempers schmaltzy material with wit and a certain dour knowingness. With another boy playing piano, David would tear off both the melody line and Bunny Berigan's solos: when we were stopped from listening in the school lunch break, one reason given was that the music being made would in some way damage the piano. The absurdity of this made martyrs of us, in particular the outraged pianist, whose parents had already chivvied and bullied him to Grade Six of the Associated Board. A compromise was reached. We might form ourselves into a club and listen to recordings.

Suddenly, it became apparent that all over school, boys in our year had parents who had saved precious shellac records of Louis Armstrong, Sidney Bechet, Benny Goodman, Ellington and others. These were brought in and played with the utmost reverence on the music teacher's gramophone. He never attended these lunchtime sessions but occasionally the headmaster could be glimpsed leaning over the balcony that ran alongside the old hall, his chin in his hands.

Jazz acted on me the way it was intended to do: joyous and angry by turns; sly, sophisticated, forgiving. Easy to grasp in its formal elements, tied since its beginning to dancing and self-expression, the music carried with it an additional freight of rebellion and – too often – personal tragedy. It was not the school's music teacher who told us how jazz players were eradicated from Nazi Germany by Goebbels but the mild and absent-minded Hollingsworth, a Fats Waller fan.

I found there was a Cambridge Jazz Club and that visiting bands appeared at the Rex Ballroom. To the scant enthusiasm that existed among the school staff could be added beery and bewhiskered men in fair-isle pullovers and agricultural corduroys, mumbling woozily on pub terraces. Some of these could easily have bored for Europe and all of them had staggering amounts of arcane knowledge.

'Died in Kansas City after a solo gig in Hollywood, the Zanzibar Room. Got on the train back to NY and all of a sudden, pffft, that was it.'

'Had his manager with him at the time, I believe, Gerry?'

'Correct, Clive. Bloke's name was Ed Kirkeby.'

Thus the demise of Fats Waller in 1943.

Jazz made America understandable. From the torrent of conflicting signals that came from that country, I had picked out the part that interested me most: the steady traffic of vibrant human-interest stories, told in an idiom as powerful as film but without, for the most part, film's saccharine sentimentality. The presumption of every film made in America was that at the end goodness triumphed and the building blocks of the story went back into the box. In jazz, by comparison, the story was left spilled on the floor, to be continued in the next instalment. For me, no torch singer in a B-movie, no matter how well lit, could even attempt 'Body and Soul' after Coleman Hawkins was done with it. Likewise, no mere picture could equal the sombre Jimmy Rushing singing

> *I left my baby*
> *Standin' in the back door cryin'*

to which the Basie orchestra added the chug-chug chords of a train pulling away, with a final despairing shout from Buck Clayton's trumpet.

At about this time, the gospel singer Mahalia Jackson was booked to appear at the No. 3 touring theatre in Cambridge. When the curtain went up, the distraught Mahalia, sitting at the piano in a green satin gown, saw that her entire audience comprised seven schoolboys. After a glance into the wings she burst into tears and the curtain came down. We climbed on to the stage and begged the theatre manager to bring her back, even for one song. Miss Jackson, as grave as she was plump, was persuaded to return. We queued up to shake her hand and then stood by the piano while she sang. When she had finished she stood, smiled a little uncertainly and then said, 'God bless you, children.' She walked off and was swallowed by the backstage dark. An elderly assistant stage manager walked on and closed the lid on the piano, buffing it absent-mindedly with his cuff.

'Okay, lads,' he said, pleasantly enough. 'Hop it.'

Chapter Seven

ONE OF THE MEMBERS OF STAFF HAD A GIRLFRIEND, a beaky-nosed Italian with a mournful face. We met by chance outside the Regal, after a Saturday-night showing of Henry King's war movie, *Twelve O'Clock High*. The teacher caught my eye while waiting for his Italian to open her tiny red umbrella. Rain washed down the street and the blocked gutters overswam the kerb.

'What did you make of that, then?'

If I wanted to be anybody that night, it was Major-General Savage, played in the film by Gregory Peck. There was no part in this story for my other screen hero, Robert Mitchum. Mitchum's world was compromised by tragically flawed women, whom he saved (or didn't) by getting down on the street, going the extra mile, strolling sleepy-eyed into seedy bars or hotel bedrooms. Mitchum had the insolent haircut, the amazingly wide shoes with paper-thin soles, above all the gaberdine suits that hung on him like academic dress. He could fight when he had to. He took the bad guy's best shot without flinching and smooched the double-crossing dame with only the slightest of ironic grimaces. More often than not he came out of the story the way he ambled into it, alone.

But Major-General Savage! Who would not wish to arrive at a failing East Anglian airbase wearing a belted raincoat and a soft American cap, his very first act to rouse the gate guard from his comic-reading lethargy? Savage was there on a mission. His predecessor and personal friend, played by Gary Merrill, loved his men too much. But this was war, and for the Mighty Eighth in particular a time of maximum effort. The decent and kindly Gregory Peck was being asked to act against his nature and turn round the fortunes of an exhausted and unlucky squadron. I watched with my hands clenched when he gathered his sullen crews together and gave it to them with the bark on. To do the job he was asking of them, they should consider themselves already dead.

Outside in the rain, the Italian woman was introduced and shook hands with me.

'Are you American?' she asked doubtfully, staring at my newly purchased zoot suit and a haircut that was known to barbers as duck's-arse.

'He'd like to be. But unfortunately he's not.'

'We'd all like to be what we're not, caro.'

All this while, a girl had been watching me from the edge of the cinema marquee. She was my own age, solid-looking but at the same time lithe and pantherish. She smiled broadly, showing faintly crooked teeth. I was still Major-General Savage and by way of response gave her my troubled eyes. At which, her boyfriend came out of the cinema and gave *me* the hard stare.

'Yeah?' he challenged.

Before I could say anything gruff and Savage-like, she slipped her arm through his and they walked away down the rippling pavement. Just before they rounded the corner, the girl turned for one last glance. *Twelve O'Clock High* dissolved like a soap bubble and I was back as Robert Mitchum, the wronged guy, the loser who was only the winner to the girl who knew the score. I strolled away, beckoned by the mean streets, down which a man has to go. The fact that I was walking to the bus station and a twopenny ticket home was, for the moment, beside the point.

It was only when I was on the bus that I realised I knew this girl slightly. I knew her nickname and that she was at the Girls' High School. Had she been smiling at me, or laughing at the zoot suit and yellow socks? It began to matter. When I got home, my mother was still up, sitting in the kitchen with her hands round the teapot.

'You look a complete gink in that get-up,' she mumbled unhelpfully.

In the bedroom, I studied myself. Cecil Gee, who tailored this suit (where else would you go in London for authentic threads?) had never intended it should be worn by a fifteen-year-old boy who did not yet tip the scales much over nine stone. Lester Young could have carried it off, as well as Dan Duryea in *Criss Cross*, in which the great bit-player did his best to upstage Burt Lancaster and Yvonne de Carlo. In certain lights, the suit would have looked good on Eighth Avenue. It would have shone in any kind of film where world-weary detectives in hats roust the hoods and take them downtown for a beating. This was a suit made for homicide on the sidewalk. In Cambridge, modelled by some skinny kid who had yet to shave, its magic was diluted. I decided gloomily that the girl outside the cinema *had* been laughing at it and even – if she had no heart at all – at my carefully modelled Mitchum hair.

I suddenly remembered where I had seen her before. The tan suit with its plunging lapels had its first outing at a dance in the Town Hall, where it cannot have been shown to best advantage. I was there as the guest of the Wrestler, who was in turn squiring his mother. That suggests it was a fund-raiser for the United Nations Association, about which she was very passionate. The Wrestler turned up wearing a blue serge suit with a school tie, I in my finger-length drape. Neither of us danced, of course. We sat on folding chairs at the edge of the crowd, commenting on big girls in taffeta and, in my case, the pure awfulness of the band. And it was then that I saw the mystery girl, at a large family table, one or two of the party in evening dress. Like me, she had taken a chance on love, and was wearing a sprigged off-the-shoulder ball gown and (as I found out much later) her mother's high-heel shoes. When I pointed her out to the Wrestler, he sniffed.

'Fifteen going on twenty-seven,' he decided. 'But nice arms.'

'Nice *arms?*'

His wrestling days were over. They had been replaced by donnish aggression, accentuated by black-framed glasses and uncombable wiry hair. I had noticed how he liked to stand with one leg advanced, his hand in his jacket pocket, with just the thumb showing – the orator about to let rip. His glare could have cut brick.

'You felt you had to come dressed like that, did you?' he asked.

'Like what?'

Shortly after, the dance ended. Going down the marble staircase, winding a scarf round her neck, the Wrestler's mother had the last word.

'Such a pity you boys are so shy. And looking so grown-up and manly, the pair of you,' she added with deft irony.

A little way outside Cambridge was Madingley Cemetery, where nearly four thousand American aircrew are buried. I had once cycled as far as the entrance before funking it. It was possible but not certain that the Ken who bought me the Philip's Atlas was buried there, though his B-17 might have been blown out of the sky anywhere over Europe. Then again, he might have flown all his missions and gone home to Indiana a hero. If it were so, who could say what kind of suit he wore nowadays, or how he combed his hair? It seemed unlikely that he looked anything like me on Saturday nights.

It was something of a crushing admission.

My other uniform was issued from a musty wooden hut at the edge of the school playground. There, hundreds of bundles of khaki and boxes of boots were stacked on shelves, the whole presided over by Mr Mansell, he who it was said had arrested Goering at pistol-point. These days his webbing belt was let out to its limit and hung under his belly in a comfortable loop. Even a moderately alert Goering could have eluded the present-day Mansell by walking away at a fast clip. For all that, the war was only five years distant and the Combined Cadet Force was taken very seriously.

On CCF days the staff wore their uniforms with easy familiarity, swooping into class like men who had just arrived by jeep from Divisional HQ. Under their martial eye, we cadets marched and drilled and learned to read maps and take compass bearings. The maps were Ordnance Survey sheets from a variety of locations in Scotland. We were asked to imagine machine-gun nests scattered in the Muir of Fowlis and a dug-in infantry platoon at every minor crossroads. Some place-names from these map-reading exercises have stuck for ever: in one, the enemy had its forces concentrated at the Glenkindie Arms Hotel. They were there in battalion strength.

We had no naval contingent but the cream of the school

was selected to join the air section, which was housed in a black hut that had once been a cricket pavilion. There they learned morse code, identified aircraft silhouettes and studied stellar navigation. Their senior NCO was a gangly prefect who flew gliders at the weekend. Once a year, the entire squadron was taken to Marshall's Aerodrome and given a go on the flight simulator, a bad-tempered piece of mechanical engineering that replicated the controls of the Tiger Moth and what happened when they were mishandled. Air cadets had no style – they were made up of the tallest, thinnest and brainiest boys in the school who wore their uniforms like lab coats – but they had fun.

Life in the infantry was less beguiling. Every summer we lurched off in elderly coaches to some woods near Thetford. There we lay in hollows, firing blanks from Lee Enfield rifles. We munched huge bully beef sandwiches and swigged dark brown tea and, like real soldiers, hung about in cursing boredom until the set-piece 'battles' of the afternoon began. In these, thunder flashes were thrown and smoke grenades hurled this way and that. The enemy comprised terrified smaller boys and those could not be trusted even with blank ammunition (Dillon). They were hidden in preselected locations deep in the fir plantations where they spent the day squabbling, reading comics or, in Dillon's case, smoking.

These field days, for all the brief noises they created, had an airy and insubstantial character. Under huge skies, we crept and crawled, giving covering fire, working dead ground, following the training manuals to the letter. But at the same time the blind persistence of nature, which had already colonised the odd bits of concrete structures left over from the war, was like a silent reproof.

'What skull is that?' someone cried, recoiling from a perfectly bleached wedge of bones. Ablett, a country boy, studied it briefly.

'That's a fox,' he replied. 'Or more like, a vixen.'

In one ponderously organised attack, I lay on my back looking at cumulus clouds building in the east, feeling my mind float away towards them like thistledown. The thin scattering of pine saplings under which I stretched barely stirred and though I was in charge of the non-existent Bren gun, the sheer emptiness of the landscape overwhelmed me, and for a few moments at any rate, I slept.

'Well now,' one of the teacher-umpires said, sitting down beside me and lighting an illicit cigarette. His name was Bert Perkins, whom we once supposed to have been the King's private detective. 'See the rest of your chaps galloping along over there? Dead as door-knockers, every one of them. I take it you see all this soldiering business as pointless, do you?'

He was mistaken. When I could bring my mind down from the clouds, I saw the wearing of uniform as the presager of coming events. Though I did not read newspapers and barely listened to reports on the radio, I could sense the generally fearful and uneasy mood in the country. What was required of we cadets, with our gaiters fastened back to front and sand grinding the bolts of our rifles, our berets flopping like cowpats, was patriotism of the crudest sort. It needed no explication, which was lucky, for there was little to be had. As it was taught to me in school, history stopped with the Reform Act of 1832. According to Mr Howell, poetry died with Masefield and the novel even earlier, with Trollope and Meredith. Geography was not even on the syllabus.

We were exceptionally well-taught boys with a fundamental problem of understanding. I think every secondary school in the country was shown film of the liberation of Belsen, watched by me at least through laced fingers. After the screening of this film we knew more – certainly at the level of moving pictures – than our parents, most of them. But what these images meant, the light they shed on all humanity's capacity for evil, was beyond us. It was a story about the fog of war, about decent men stumbling across nightmare horrors in the dark. We knew nothing of the gulags, nor the de-humanised nature of Uncle Joe. We thought we knew the benefits the British Empire had bestowed upon the world, without once thinking of its victims.

Only once a year did the patriotism demanded of us come into sharp focus. Every Remembrance Day, on the stroke of eleven, the CCF mounted an honour guard in the school yard. The entire school was mustered for a three-minute silence. Some of the senior boys – the sergeants and sergeant-majors who selected and trained this double file – could perhaps see the shadow cast by coming events more clearly than the rest of us. In the late summer of 1950, the Korean War began. National service in Britain was extended to two years.

It occurred to me one day that I could cure myself of the lonesome cowboy blues I felt engulfing me by cycling to London, a distance of about fifty miles. Told about this plan, my mother merely shrugged and lit another cigarette. The only question she had was who would feed the rabbits, my father's latest attempt to teach us discipline and responsibility. The poor creatures lived in a hutch he had knocked up on one of his weekend visits. Watching him humming contentedly, a pencil behind his ear, I knew that the carpentry was far more important to him than the animals that would live there. When finished, the hutch wanted for nothing except a chimney and a letter-box. As for the occupants, he had no more interest in them than we did.

'It's the principle of the thing,' he explained sourly, in a phrase that was fast becoming his signature tune. No rabbits in England had finer accommodation but when he was finished, he walked indoors and never spoke of them again. (When my brother Neil was asked to name the rabbits – there were two of them – he simply stared at the creatures in a zen-like way before wandering off down the garden.)

The bike that would take me to London had no gears and was of a style called roadster: upright handlebars, hugely heavy frame, tin mudguards. Rust had claimed the wheel rims. Once – thanks to a postwar interest in speedway – the kind of bike a boy had was of the greatest importance. The best examples were customised – the front wheel smaller in circumference than the back, sweep-around handlebars made from iron tubing, coloured adhesive taping applied wherever it could be wound. Charlie, the boy down the road who was rebuilding a motor-cycle, had even invented a form of front-wheel suspension, a system by which the wheel floated free of the forks and was held to them by drilled bars and fat cylinder springs taken from bedsteads. Later on, the craze was to scour rubbish tips to find sit-up-and-beg handlebars and turn them upside down to give the look of a racing bike. (In 1949, Fausto Coppi won the Giro d'Italia and the Tour de France in the same season, an amazing feat of athletic endurance. It started a minor Coppi craze.)

But the very latest fad was to forswear anything ostentatious. The older the bike and the more wrecked, the better. Mine qualified handsomely. The rear mudguard was broken in two and tied together with wire; there was a spoke missing in the front wheel; and the brake blocks were worn down to the metal. With this trendily ugly machine, I set off one morning along the A10. It was midweek and in places the road was mysteriously empty for minutes on end. For the first ten miles or so I felt myself among friends, as if the traffic that passed knew me for a local. This comforting thought gradually evaporated. I was out there on my own.

I had gambled on the weather and when it began to

drizzle I had nothing but a sweater to keep me dry. The harvest was gathered in and the stubble fields I passed had a faintly sour look to them, as though the countryside was a resentful elder relative. Men dressed in the cast-offs of war – small men, with tight-shut faces – coaxed tractors out of side roads, or dug drainage. If they looked up at all as I clattered past, hair plastered to my skull, it was with a distinctly unfriendly expression. Never mind a bit of rain, they seemed to be saying. Look at us here. See what you get for crawling on your hands and knees up Monte Cassino, or jumping out of a plane in Holland?

I broke the journey halfway, climbing through a blackthorn hedge to sit and eat biscuits and drink dandelion and burdock from a bottle I had carried inside my shirt. Hertfordshire is not famous for its mountains but the landscape had definitely clenched up. I got back on my bike bearing it real hate, pedalling slowly up inclines and freewheeling gratefully down the other side. The sun came out. Ware was sleepy and comfortable and Broxbourne not without its charms. But at Cheshunt the anthill quality of London life began. At Enfield it intensified and by the time I reached Tottenham I counted myself lucky to be in one piece.

Looking back on it, my parents must have been mad to let me make this trip. I had no map, wore no special clothes and carried less than half a crown in my pocket. I recently looked up a London A–Z to see what route I should have taken once I hit the urban sprawl. The A10 peters out (from a swede's point of view) at Stamford Hill, though pressing on down the length of Kingsland Road would have brought me at last to Bishopsgate, where I could have crossed the river at, say, Southwark Bridge. This I never did. Instead, I turned west in Tottenham and fumbled my way to Turnpike Lane, where the tube station had a comforting curve to it and at least half the appearance of a cinema. Then began a long and bumpy slog through Harringay to Seven Sisters Road, which Christopher Hibbert has described as 'a long straggling road through dingy suburbs' without mentioning that it has, for the cyclist from Cambridge, the advantage of being largely downhill.

I chose this lengthy diversion for a very good reason, for in Camden Town I intersected the Number 3 bus route which ran past the end of Lambeth Walk. All I had to do now was to follow along – or, more accurately, be overtaken by – buses coughing their way through central London via Piccadilly Circus, Trafalgar Square and Whitehall, before crossing the Thames at Lambeth Bridge.

Today I would not from choice drive any part of the way in a car. But then I pedalled along with my mind, as it were, floating a few inches above my head. My wrists ached more than my legs, my back groaned and I saw the road through eyes red-rimmed by grit and fumes. There was a mild panic when the sun began to lower and whole sections of the road ahead lay bathed in dingy rose. When I finally fell off my bike outside Jockie's tiny shop I had been riding for nearly nine hours. My grandparents welcomed me by cooking egg and chips and, as an afterthought, pressing a bottle of stout into my hands.

'So you never come down Stamford Hill way?' Jockie asked. 'Well, you missed a trick there and that's no lie. Does your father know you're here?'

'He's come to see *us*,' Queenie said, lathering me another slice of bread and marge, passing it across on the blade of the bread-knife. But in her eyes and the set of her mouth I could see she was thinking that, like my mother, I was not the complete one pound note. Not by a long shot.

That summer, my father taught me to swim by throwing me in at the deep end of the outdoor pool at Jesus Green. It was an overdue lesson, for I went there usually with no intention of getting wet. The purpose of undressing and dragging on a costume was to sit on the grass and watch girls sunbathe. Once in a while this or that young woman would climb the ladder to the diving boards. Before launching themselves, they would pluck briefly at the hem of their swimsuits, a gesture I found intensely erotic.

One Saturday afternoon my father said he would come with me to the pool. For a while he sat peaceably enough, in flannels and an Aertex shirt, completing the *Daily Telegraph* crossword, a test of intelligence he understood and approved. He filled in the clues with a silver propelling pencil and had got to the point where he liked to time himself from start to finish. He used the wristwatch he had worn over Arnhem, its glass a cloudy yellow, and while he worked he hummed tunelessly.

The *Telegraph* crossword was an importation from his new office life, about which I knew nothing. Completing it was a huge achievement for a man who had left school at twelve and whose first job had been with a decorating gang, whose contract it was to paint LCC school blackboards black. He had every right to be proud of himself. That day, he asked me the answer to various clues seconds before providing the solution himself, chuckling. I was, and still am, blind to crossword puzzles. I sulked beside him, my head on my knees.

'Not going in?' he asked several times.

I should have been more alert. Quite suddenly, he laid down his paper, dragged me to my feet and hurled me into the greeny water.

I flailed about in blind panic, feeling hands snatch at me and other people's skin slide across mine. In the mêlée, I clashed heads with someone and for the only time in my life saw stars, real Christmas tree stars. I was at last hauled to the side by a very large and indignant woman in a frilled rubber bathing cap. When I got out and coughed up what I had swallowed on to the concrete slabs of the pool surround, my father had already left and was cycling home, mission accomplished.

'What kind of a girl are you?' he needled me at supper

that night. 'Can't swim, can't mend the simplest thing in the
house, can't fix your own bloody bike.'

'Rode it to London though,' my mother said, sly.

He laid down his knife and fork.

'When?' he asked.

I realised that Queenie had not told him. When nobody
spoke, he pushed his plate away, his jaw jumping. My mother
laughed.

'He didn't go there because he was missing *you*,' she
scoffed.

Just before my marriage, eight years into the future, I
worked in a nursery, growing carnations for the early-
morning Covent Garden market. The six people I joined
there distressed me at first – it seemed incredible that people
who met daily with nothing but each other's company for
entertainment should spend their time jibing, harbouring old
grudges and fantasising about their real selves. It was only
when going home one night that I realised what was being
mirrored here – it was the story of my parents' marriage. By
1950 they had come to an unbreachable logjam of emotions,
in which the cause of their misery was receding into the past
but its consequences could never be resolved. All that was left
was the bickering, at which they excelled.

The spark had gone out of my mother and with it any
hope she might have had of changing her life. She was hardly
forty years old and only halfway through her time on earth.
But the game was up. Once, her manic moods had seemed to

promise a break-out of some kind. She was leaving, she would announce to me. There were people in London who still remembered her (a particularly empty boast) but then again, maybe she'd go further. She would even, if she felt like it, go abroad.

'Where?' I asked, bewildered.

'Where none of you lot will ever find me,' she promised.

These days, she was more like a ship that was sinking. She bought all her clothes at jumble sales, even her shoes, and from being careful with her hair and make-up, went for days without washing. Her hearing grew worse. She was of course in deep depression and should have seen a doctor. Any suggestion of that was received with terror. The only doctor she had ever met had signed the piece of paper that had sent her to an asylum. I suppose we must have been registered with a practice – was it a law of the land, even? – but I had no idea of its name or location.

Materially, my brother did not suffer. But I could sometimes see him struggling to understand. She talked to him a lot, as once she had talked to me. My father had filled the house with toys and these lay scattered about the floor for weeks on end. At mealtimes he ate slowly and methodically, watched by her with a fanatical intensity. One of the benefits of having Neil in the world was that the bathroom was used more often. A wall heater was installed and the immersion boiler rewired. Neil would sit in the bath, sucking water from the casing of a tin submarine, smiling with what sometimes seemed to me preternatural calm. At bedtime he went to sleep at once, his hands lax on the pillow, his face untroubled.

If I had not been such a callow youth, which most certainly I had become, perhaps I could have done more to help Peggy. It is hard to know what, for by now we were all in fixed positions, without the slightest chance of altering. She and I squabbled over the smallest things, my father and I were open enemies. And when they looked at me they saw a preposterous figure, neither man nor boy, and a monster of selfishness into the bargain.

That year, the worst thing possible happened. I was back in London, mooching about in the little bike shop, on this particular day mending a puncture for a customer who was going to call back later. Jockie was in the yard, pouring diluted horseshit on to his tiny raised borders. From the parlour I heard a huffing noise which Queenie sometimes made when clearing the grate of ashes. I carried on springing the tyre back over the wheel rim using tyre levers taken from a display card. If they were scratched, then so be it, for who had last come in to buy a tyre lever? And anyway I was bored by the Walk and its too simple morality. The night before, Jockie had chastised me for cycling to London earlier in the year and never seeing my dad, a piece of blind bleeding impertinence the like of which he'd never have thought possible from one of the family, no, never. I looked over at

Queenie to see what she thought and instead of contradicting her partner, she gave a little unsmiling shrug.

I threw down the tyre levers and glanced into the parlour. She was not cleaning the grate but lay on her face, fighting for her life. I tried to pull her over, shocked that she had wet herself. My shouts brought in Jockie from the yard.

'Run and fetch the doctor,' he said.

'Where?'

'Lambeth North Road. Near Sid the barber's.'

Like a fool, I did as he asked, haring across the road and running until my lungs burned. The doctor's surgery was easy enough to find but the dusty brown door was shut.

'He ain't there,' a passing woman said.

I banged a few times and then ran all the way back to the Walk. The one time in my life when I was called upon to do something important, I had done exactly the wrong thing.

When I got back, the door to the shop was wide open and the parlour empty. Irrationally, I ran to see if they were in the yard and then tore upstairs on the same fruitless search. Across the street was a bakery run by an Italian family. When I stumbled back into the shop, frantic, a woman in her thirties was standing there. She was dressed all in black, like the Angel of Death.

'We call the ambulance,' she explained, not quite able to keep the reproach out of her voice. 'Grandma 'as gone to 'ospital.'

'Where's Jockie?'

She laid a hand on my bare arm.

'You done what you could. Want me to stay with you?'

I shook my head. I realised I had earlier pushed my way through a dozen neighbours who had been alerted by the ambulance bell. The front rank of these was peering in on us.

'It's Bert's boy,' someone confirmed in a matter-of-fact voice.

I sat down on the shop floor and howled. 'I did the wrong thing!'

What I should have done was passing through my brain like moving pictures: the phone boxes by the Lambeth Baths, the 999 call, the cushioning of Queenie's head, the call for help from neighbours, passers-by, anyone. The good-natured Italian woman knelt in front of me, holding my face in her hands, while the deepest self-loathing I have ever experienced rose from my gut in aching sobs.

'Calma,' she said. When she pulled me to my feet, my hand hit her soft and rounded breast and she smiled absent-mindedly. 'Do you got a hankie?'

'What should I do now?'

'You could ring your dad.'

'I don't know his number.'

'No? Then nothing.'

I laid my head on the shop bench, weeping.

'He's took it hard,' a voice said.

When I looked round they had all gone. There was a terrible caramel stink coming from somewhere. Potatoes on the huge old-fashioned gas stove in the scullery had boiled away to nothing, their remains stuck to the saucepan in a black and brown mess. I threw the red-hot pan into the yard and sat on the wall of Jockie's border, my head in my hands, my throat raw from crying.

An hour later the shop bell went. Jim came in, half-carrying my grandfather, already shrunk to a caricature of the little bantam man who had slogged it out in this house for so many years. He sat Jockie in the chair that was his and only his and, horrified, I watched the old man's head fall forward on to the table with a sickening thud.

'Go and make us a cup of tea,' Jim said quietly, the calm in his voice as wide as an ocean.

I was watching the kettle boil when he came into the scullery. He put his arm round me with such compassion that I knew at once what he was going to say. I burst out crying all over again.

'She's gone,' he murmured, ruffling my hair. Then, like a barber, he took my chin in his hand and made me lift my head and look into his eyes.

'There's nothing anyone could have done. She died in the ambulance.'

Another hour passed, in which Jim rolled his father a cigarette and held him in his arms while he smoked it. I sat there beyond all tears, shivering as if I were in fever. Jim pushed his little tin rolling machine towards me.

'Make yourself a smoke, and buck up, there's a good boy.'

A little while after my father arrived by cab, wearing a brown suit and coming, it seemed to me, from another planet.

Neither my mother nor I attended the funeral. Queenie is buried in Peckham and I have never seen the grave. It was agreed that Jockie, like King Lear, would share the rest of the year with his sons, moving from one to another until he could find his feet again. He died only a few months afterwards and if ever it could be said that a man died of a broken heart, that was his fate. Once again, my mother and I were not present at the funeral. The stock in the shop, the magical properties of which had entranced me all those years, was sold for £40. In time the house itself was pulled down. My Aunt Jessie, who knew what honour was and how history works, climbed over the rubble and retrieved a ridge tile from the roof. It was the gesture of a believer.

Chapter Eight

IN 1951, THE EXISTING EXAMINATION SYSTEM FOR secondary education was abolished and replaced by the General Certificate of Education. I began living in the looming shadow of the first-ever O-levels. They were discussed much as fearful alpine villagers might mention the word avalanche. It was agreed early on by the school that every boy in the fifth form should sit the examination in ten subjects, the better to gauge how to proceed in subsequent years. The blither members of staff said we had nothing to fear from this bold scheme. Others looked forward with more or less open pleasure at the prospect of our being slaughtered. The national consensus seemed to be that if the papers were marked as it was thought they would be, five passes would constitute the minimum of success. We, with our proud ambition to sit ten subjects, were like the forlorn hope, the regiment that volunteers itself for certain death.

Mrs Broom's ancient admonition that I should metticilate came home to roost. Many a dull afternoon, it pecked at the classroom windows like a raven. I reviewed my position as unwilling candidate. Short of pornography – and perhaps not even then – it seemed impossible to fail art, which was taught by a genial man with a mauve silk tie, who was also one of the few jazzers on the staff. (I understood his dictum that any fool thinks he can paint but extended it hopefully to mean any fool thinks he is a judge of painting and will accordingly return a fool's opinion.) Other subjects were more problematic. It was widely held that biology was a soft subject. I gave myself next to no hope of passing chemistry or physics, however, nor was it very likely that I would hit a gambler's lucky streak with maths. Yet maths was a must-have pass. I agonised further. A fool that daydreamed about being Robert Mitchum was not especially qualified to come to grips with *Macbeth* but he did have imagination at his disposal, however warped. Robert Mitchum among the bunsen burners was another matter; nor did he find himself entirely at home in the impedimenta train in Gaul, divide the province any way you liked.

I consulted the Wrestler. We took the same walk to Grantchester that my father and I had taken during the war. It was bitterly cold and frost spiked the dead grass in the meadows. He was a less than sympathetic companion. One of his recent affectations was a Basque beret, a piece of revolutionary headgear that went with underground printing presses and clandestine meetings in cellars. He smoked Gauloises.

'I can't bother myself about a few unimportant exams,' he

said grandly as we tramped along. ' I'm going to university and that's it.'

'You are?'

'Well, of course. Where else are the levers?'

We stopped for a smoke under a pollarded willow and watched thin shims of ice go past on the river. All the colour in his face had fled to his ears, which burned bright red. He could see I wanted to ask him about the levers. I did; but nothing on earth would make me utter the question out loud. It was a movie moment.

'Look,' he said at last. 'You don't like school. I can see its limitations, too. But it's just school. In a couple of years' time I am going to be where the real power is.'

His beret was worn with a devilish lack of insouciance, the leather edging straight across his frown. Round his neck was an immense wool scarf such as my mother might have knitted. We looked into each other's eyes. I was determined to stare him down but not before he had a chance to reflect on our brief history of lust, some of which had taken place on the other side of the river, not far from where we stood. After a tense silence, he reached out and took my hand in both of his.

'I shan't forget you,' he promised.

'That's nice to know.'

This flippancy wounded him. He said so. I flicked my butt into the Cam, something I knew was guaranteed to annoy him.

'Well, is that all there is to you?' he shrilled suddenly. 'Charlie Parker and Danny Kaye?'

'You've missed out Ella Fitzgerald. And Stan Kenton.'

'Don't you get it? It's all *crap*. You're walking in your sleep.'

Dizzy Gillespie had a beret. Thelonius Monk had some kind of skull cap. Bill Basie was fond of a jaunty yachting number. Lester Young I imagined slept in his dove-grey borsalino. Was the music they made really of such little consequence? Moreover, I resented the Wrestler's imputation that I did not like school. To my very great surprise, Mr Howell had nominated me for the A. B. Mayne English Prize, named after a previous headmaster and not lightly given away. Cambridge United had about as much chance of winning the FA Cup as my lifting the A. B. Mayne but, as my mother would have put it, it was the thought that counted. The truth of the matter was that I liked school all the more for seeing its benign influence – in Howell's case, his infinite patience and good manners – approach the end.

Every Saturday we jazz fans gathered in Miller's Music Shop, where the listening booths were downstairs, overseen by an elderly man and a woman with vinegar in her veins. Their battle was to prevent more than four of us crowding into a cubicle at any one time. The shop kept no jazz in stock and our selections were made from the Capitol catalogue, or reviews in obscure magazines. Very sensibly, the management had a policy of demanding half the money up front, so that Saturdays were made all the more exciting: what had been ordered as long as a month ago was then played for the first time, with the added thrill that you were going to have to pay the balance whether you liked the record or not. It was jazz as cargo cult.

(Forty years later, I was in a jazz store at Third and Market, Philadelphia, where all the recordings I coveted in those golden days were readily available remastered in CD format, arranged alphabetically in glistening banks. I bought a hundred and fifty dollars' worth of arcana from the 1940s and 1950s and carried them proudly to the clerk, who was black. His job was to write them up in a sales ledger and I waited expectantly for him to raise his eyes and acknowledge a true believer. He did look up, but only to say, 'Dag, man, whassamatta wit you? These people are *deee-ad*.')

Saturday mornings at Miller's were a social occasion. Girls were never invited but drifted down in two and threes to watch half a dozen absurd schoolboys nodding their heads and going *Tch-tchi da! tch-tchi da! da-doo-ba, tooosh!!!* while Vinegar Lady banged in four-four time on the cubicle door. Perhaps only in youth can one leave a record store after a couple of hours' devotions and be amazed that it is still light outside and that the world has in it such reprehensible ordinariness – cars, buses, shoppers and, in Cambridge, bicycles flocking like house-martins.

I had a second, newer passion. On Saturdays there was

a market in front of the Shire Hall, selling fruit and veg, clothes and shoes. On the Great St Mary's side of the square, a second-hand bookseller had a stall of waifs and lost souls I had begun to browse. The books on Mr David's stall could be bought for sixpence or a shilling and the stock included many dishevelled Penguins. The first of these I ever bought was J. R. Ackerley's *Hindoo Holiday*, decorated on the back cover with an advertisement for 'Army Club, The Front Line Cigarette'. A hearty-looking officer, who would probably have shot Ackerley out of hand had he ever met him, is seen smoking a Front Line. His endorsement runs beneath: 'This is the cigarette for the fellow with a full-size man's job to do. When you're feeling all hit up, it steadies the nerves.'

The first six words of *Hindoo Holiday* are these: 'He wanted someone to love him.' The pronoun in the sentence indicates the Maharaja of Chhockrapur, a state invented by Ackerley (though the prince was real enough) and the someone he wanted to love him was a man. 'When I first heard your name,' the Maharaja tells his new secretary coyly, 'it made me think of a stream of water running over little stones.' Penguin marketed this book as Travel and Adventure and the ploy worked, at least as far as some indolent RAF education officer was concerned. My copy had been sent to amuse the boys at Wireless Station SW76, Ismailia, as shown by a box stamp on the inside cover.

But then again, Penguin No. 48 was *A Passage to India*, the author of which had preceded Ackerley to Chhockrapur and passed on the secretary's job to him. This work was also to be found on David's stall – and for all I knew, E. M. Forster, a very short walk from King's, may have been standing next to me in the flesh when I passed my money across.

In the Wrestler's view, indiscriminate book-buying, based on price alone, qualified as sleepwalking just as much as collecting jazz. I had thought to impress him with tales of dusty tomes and broken-backed heroes laid low by time. He squelched me by explaining that he bought *his* books new at Heffer's, strictly on the basis of their content. When I asked him how he could afford to do that, he gave me his Lenin fifty-metre stare and said that his parents footed the bill. Bourgeois revisionists they might be but at heart they were just as keen as he on seeing the ruling class overthrown. Their investment would then be repaid a hundred times over.

'When you're an MP?'

'When the whole House of Commons farce has been swept away.'

'Where do you stand on the farce of the university system, or shouldn't I ask?'

One frosty morning in 1951, I saw a familiar stooped figure standing in front of David's bookstall, reading. It was Mr Hollingsworth, wearing a mac that came down to his shins and, like the Wrestler, a beret. But Hollingsworth's beret did not perch like a dinner plate. It was filled with skull and its pleasing roundness gave him the appearance of a cheerful watchmaker. He held up the book he was holding for me to scan the cover.

'If you tell me this isn't very much needed on the voyage I think I shall give up the business of teaching altogether.' He pushed the book into my hands. 'No, no, I want you to have it. You are holding work by a master of the English language.'

He had not taught me since the third form and I was shocked to see how old and grey he seemed. He smiled diffidently.

'Mr Howell tells me you have become quite the wag.'

'He's never said that to me.'

'No,' he agreed. 'I was merely trying to put the best construction possible on some passing remarks of his. So, this O-level business. Do you think you might get by with it? In English, I mean?'

My heart froze. Hollingsworth, hearing his dagger grind against bone, chuckled, patted me on the back and piked off down the pavement. Characteristically, while presenting me with my copy of *Right Ho, Jeeves*, he had forgotten to pay for it, something Mr David pointed out in the most economical way by holding out a mittened claw.

To my very great surprise, my father took a late interest in my school career. It began by indirection: he came to watch me play for the Second XV a couple of times. Though he had never taken part in competitive sport in his life – other than thrashing his twin brother in amateur boxing finals – he felt free to advise me on the tactics of rugby football. Ever the quick study, he placed himself on the touchline next to Mr Eckersley. What he learned from him, he passed on to me.

'Too much kicking. You've got to get the ball out faster and flatter. Get those backs moving.'

I resented being told how to play a game he knew nothing of, but looking back on it, I realise he was showing me one way to succeed in life: always stand next to the man who does know what he's talking about. He and Eckersley unexpectedly hit it off: my father had the Mancunian's war record out of him with the deftness of a pickpocket and they walked back down Hills Road together swapping stories. When I passed them on my bike, Eckersley was doubled over with laughter: he had just heard the one about meeting Eisenhower. What made it funny in his eyes was doubtless the image of a chippy Tommy, as my father liked to be called these days, squaring up to the suspicious-eyed Top Yank. Duckboards had been laid for Ike, which the crews occupied, making the Supreme Commander wade through mud like glue.

Tommy's other office soubriquet was AJT. It had the snap of business about it and – we had a telephone installed in the Cambridge house by now – he would sometimes absent-mindedly answer a local call by barking out his initials. It was all of a piece with his suits and Parker pens, his highly polished shoes. He bought his pipes at Dunhill's and had settled on Three Nuns as his tobacco of choice. One of the images I have of him is of teasing out the little roundels in the palm of his hand, his mind racing ahead of his stroking thumb. It was easy to picture him doing this at a busy desk, with wall planners and map overlays bouncing the light back from neon tubes, his attention filled by some recent secret memo. In recent months he had come to Cambridge for his weekends toting a leather briefcase. It had his initials stamped in gold above the lock.

What interested him most about O-levels (to which he presently turned his attention) was the idea of being examined in ten separate subjects. It was taken for granted by him that I would – *must* – pass all ten. I am guessing here but it seems pretty certain that he was moving among colleagues for whom the subject of O-levels was a canteen topic. If there were to be such things, then *his* son would outdo everybody else's or he would know the reason why. Useless to protest that he was taking this interest in me too late in the day. When I explained the problems I was having with chemistry, for example, he went straight to the remedy. Hanging his suit jacket over the back of the chair, he sat down with the textbook and, starting at page one, taught himself enough to teach me. What had taken me five years to fear and detest, he mastered in three months.

These sessions were the closest I had ever been to him both physically and emotionally. I saw him suddenly for what he was: an intensely gifted man with an insatiable hunger to be admired. Now, instead of turning down his lip at everything I said, he spent a part of each weekend coaching me.

He saw at once that I lacked any competence in mathematics and the teaching of chemistry gave way to trying to get me to respond to number and scale. We sat side by side at the otherwise unused dining-room table struggling to understand each other.

'Get your head out of your hands. You can't think if you're slouched like some poof in front of a mirror.'

'Is that what poofs do?'

But he was impervious to sarcasm. His own posture was straight-backed and alert. His hair was clipped short, his moustache trimmed to a military correctness. While the faithful Dunhill was cooling its bowl in one of my mother's brass ashtrays, he would light a Capstan Full Strength, squinting at my scratched figures through clouds of pale blue smoke. It was not in his nature to suffer fools gladly.

'You could do this if your life depended on it,' he said at the end of one afternoon. 'That's been your problem. You've had it too easy.'

This novel view of how I lived stunned me like a flying brick. I looked at him closely. He was utterly serious. When he saw the colour rising in my cheeks, he laughed.

'You're not going to tell me you don't already know that?'

He had risen in the planning department to several grades above his expected ceiling and was destined to go much further still. Within narrow limits, he could think originally, finding answers to even the most complex problems by what he called 'using his loaf'. He was competing with recent graduates in his department but had something they may have lacked. He was a believer. Everything worthwhile was part of, or the consequence, of a progression. Things could be made to fit. This was how he had built Queenie her television set and it also explained his value to Post Office Engineering. His sense of order in the material world was dazzling. Only in personal relationships had things gone wrong. This – the sort of work we were engaged in – was his solace in life.

I wanted to please him and in a deeper sense wanted him to love me. The means – some wild stabs and slices at the world of numbers – was beyond me.

'It's like watching a cow with a shovel,' he said, hissing through his teeth in delight as I mangled yet another algebraic equation.

'I can't do it and that's that.'

His laughter disappeared and a hand closed over my forearm in a sudden tight grip.

'Never let me hear you say that, understand? Never.'

My mother was jealous of these afternoons. It amused her to play the radio at maximum volume and when that failed to send Neil into the garden to dance outside the french windows, banging a tin drum I had bought him for Christmas. O-levels meant as much to her as the Continental Shelf. She assumed I would be at work by the end of the summer and spent her best wit on trying to imagine anyone in their right mind employing me. I could get seasonal work pulling turnips, or as the sweeper in some Cairo brothel, maybe. Some of her suggestions were ingenious: I could model cardigans for knitting patterns or appear as the weakling in before-and-after advertisements for chest expanders.

In the early spring I met the mystery girl again, this time face to face. She was coming out of Boots as I was walking past and she barged into my shoulder with a joky force. Flustered, I took her to Joe Lyons.

Like the Maharaja of Chhockrapur, my needs were very simple. This girl, whom I shall name Figgie, was the unlucky lightning rod for all the undischarged feelings I had about life. Every tiny gesture she made, every movement of her hands or eyes, acted on me like a spell. If she had sat there bathed from head to toe in St Elmo's fire I could not have been more amazed by her.

'You know Ginny Waites,' she opened, with a half-smile.

'Pete Dillon's girlfriend, yes.'

'Pete says you're nuts.'

'I am.'

'Do you think she's good-looking?'

'Ginny? No.'

She laughed her rich croaky laugh. 'You *are* nuts. Where's your suit today?'

'I've lent it to Dirk Bogarde.'

She nodded. *The Blue Lamp* had come out the previous year and she picked up the ironic allusion with perfect casualness. I seemed to be breathing helium.

'I have to go soon,' she murmured.

It was a clear invitation to get on with it. My heart banged wildly. I searched for the perfect response.

'You have grey eyes,' I managed to mumble.

'Is that bad?'

'Can I walk you to the bus stop or something?'

She did up her coat and smiled her crooked smile.

'I was thinking of going to the pictures tonight.'

'Alone?'

'Would I tell you if I was going with someone else? You nit.'

The film we saw was *Lullaby of Broadway*, a revue-style picture in which Doris Day goes to seek her mother in New York and finds, additionally, Gene Nelson. It was perfect. Figgie wore a grey sweater and I can't remember what kind of skirt. Her tweed overcoat was folded inside out over her knees and it was on this that our hands rested, hot and clammy. From time to time I stole a glance at her, her lips parted in a half-smile as daffy but determined Doris batted her eyelids and did her hick double-take on that practised New York sophisticate, Gene. He didn't stand a chance. I had played a match that afternoon and felt drowsy, magnificent and in love. It took all my scant reserves of common sense not to blurt that out.

When we came outside, she kissed me on the cheek.

'What is that smell?' she asked conversationally.

'Germolene. On my knee. You know.'

Her smile burst over me like a star shell.

'I really like you,' she said. When I kissed her, her mouth tasted of plums.

'I have to get the bus,' she explained. 'And you probably know I'm going with someone else. From Soham.'

'A country boy.'

'With a car. And a trial bike. You know, brrm brrm.'

'Hundred octane.'

We kissed again. Then, before I could say another thing, she disengaged herself. She pulled a woollen tam-o'-shanter from her coat and jammed it on her head.

'See you.'

'Yes, see you.'

She came back for one last peck.

'You dope,' she said with affection.

And then she was gone.

In one technicolour evening, I had crossed into my mother's territory. She winkled the story out of me after AJT had gone for the train the next day. We sat in the front room with our feet up on the furniture, sipping Camp Coffee. The detail about the Germolene sent her into fits of cackling laughter.

'She probably thought you had piles. And this other bloke. How old's he, with his car and all that? I bet she's got her feet under the table in Soham all right. Those bloody swedes, if they see a girl that shows out, the way you say she does, they're already planning the wedding.'

'She's sixteen.'

'There's a lot that can happen when you're sixteen,' she said darkly. But when I tried to describe the clothes Figgie had worn, she cheered up.

'Those tweed coats are all the rage,' she said. 'Is she tall, this girl?'

'She's not short.'

'And why do they call her Figgie?'

'It's her nickname.'

Peggy waggled her eyebrows at me. 'You've got it bad,' she said.

'I never intended to tell you any of this.'

'No, I bet you never. You lucky little sod.'

The next day, I met Dillon in the school cycle sheds. News travelled fast. His girl, Ginny Waites, had told him the whole story as relayed to her by Figgie in a telephone marathon. He shook his head at me with withering pity.

The following weekend I rang Figgie. Her father said she was out. He asked me who was calling. There was the rumble of conversation and dog barks in the background.

'Do you know when she'll be in?' I havered.

Beside me in the phone box Ginny Waites pushed her face into the sleeve of my coat to stifle her laughter.

'Tell me your name and I'll get her to call you back,' Figgie's Dad suggested briskly.

'Um-er . . .'

Busy man, he put the phone down on me. Ginny let it all

go, howling with laughter. Her breasts pushed me back against the glass and she leaned her head into my chest.

'You really *are* nuts,' she said.

Right there in the middle of Drummer Street, where Robert Mitchum had been wont to loiter, I kissed her on the lips. She kissed me back lingeringly, her arms round my neck.

'Do you want me to tell her?'

'About this?'

'No,' she shrieked. 'That you fancy her!'

This, then, was how it worked. Everything that you did not like in life could be spat out, like gristle. In its place was another, parallel life that had nothing to do with parents, or school, or films in which it was always raining and the tough guy lay watching the neon signs from some seedy hotel bed. In this other existence there was sex; and freedom greater than the Wrestler could ever imagine. All I had to do was step across, like joining the ship that had been ghosting up beside me all the time just out of the corner of my eye.

'Tell her she's perfect,' I commanded. Ginnie smiled, rubbing my nose with her forefinger.

'I'll tell her,' she said, opening the door to the phone box and stepping out with a blown kiss.

The day after my sixteenth birthday, the King opened the Festival of Britain by attending a service in St Paul's Cathedral and afterwards crossing the river to a concert at the Festival Hall. George VI had less than a year to live. A hundred years earlier the Great Exhibition had opened in Hyde Park, inside a fairy-tale glass palace. It was brought to the public under the personal direction of the Prince Consort in the teeth of great criticism and had turned out a triumph. The 1951 Festival could not help but draw unfavourable comparisons. Exceptional spring rain had set back the Battersea Pleasure Gardens by a month and the Festival Hall itself was barely finished to time. It seems doubtful that the King sensed a new spirit of the age about, such as the organisers were trying to promote. He took his cue about how things were, one presumes, from the weekly audience he gave his prime minister.

There the news was grey indeed. The Labour Government was hanging by a thread, its position not improved by the death of Ernest Bevin on 14 April, nor the resignations of Aneurin Bevan and Harold Wilson a fortnight later. These had come about for a famous reason – the imposition of health service charges to help pay for defence spending. The Government was split top to bottom and in the general election that followed six months later, Labour was turned out of office. Certainly the immediate postwar era was coming to an end but whether something new and hopeful was being ushered in was another matter.

I went to the Festival on a school trip and a second time with my father. His reaction was interesting. I sensed he was impressed against his will. There was too much of the clever sod about many of the exhibits in the Dome of Discovery and in his opinion the Festival Hall would be dead in the water before the year was out, for want of patrons. If there was a point to the Skylon he failed to see it. But the general idea had his grudging respect. If he was not any more enthusiastic, it was perhaps because he knew what I did not: that in 1951 over two hundred acres of the City of London alone still lay in complete ruin from bomb damage. Post Office Engineering had a base in Aldersgate Street to which he had been posted. He liked to walk about any new area and so discovered that to the east and north of his office, where once there had been houses and churches, there was now nothing but rubble and weeds. This wasteland extended from the east end of St Paul's all the way to the Barbican.

My grandparents' death had broken a link with what Jockie liked to describe as Ogorbli London. My father spent some time on our visit trying to reconstruct what had been knocked down to make the South Bank: much of what was described in the brochures as derelict property had formed part of his childhood landscape. He was especially interested in the retention of the Shot Tower. He half wanted to scoff at the idea of keeping it as nancy-boy sentimentalism but stood for a long time staring up. He did this so intently that others joined us.

His sister-in-law's food and a sedentary job had filled out the gallant navigator's frame. Watching him poke about the Festival site, I saw a stolid and faintly dusty-looking man with rounding shoulders. Peacetime ambition had given him the rank and salary he was looking for but had at the same time stolen something from him. He had lost his hunger. More than once he shot his cuff to look at his watch and I knew this was a recent tic, made not because he was short of time but more that time was passing him by unregarded. He was hardly growing old – he would live another forty years – but maybe he sensed the treadmill under his feet for the first time.

It happened that our visit to the Festival coincided with that of a small official party, of men in black coats and spongebag trousers, all of them sporting furled umbrellas. At a guess they were senior civil servants, raffish men with smilingly stiff manners. At their centre was a man in a lounge suit, identifiable by his accent as Australian. My father caught his eye. It was clear that he would have liked to have rescued this 'real' person from the clutches of his minders for the day, with their drawl and their habit of pointing to things with an umbrella. For a moment I thought he would actually step forward and take control, introducing himself as AJT, formerly of the RAF. The Australian, seeing himself quizzed in this way by a complete stranger, chose the coward's way out and raised a hand in greeting. My father nodded and immediately turned his back.

We did not buy, as I suggested, the expensive ice-creams on sale at the Festival site but walked back over the river to Villiers Street by the side of Charing Cross Station. There we sat in Dickensian half-light, drinking tea out of chipped mugs.

'What a bloody country this is,' my father muttered. Though he was wearing his office suit and a new raincoat, the patrons of this little café saw him at once for who he was: a Londoner who was also a displaced person. The tetchiness with which he had been born was now a common point of view: the Blitz had made heroes – and corpses – of thousands of ordinary people but in the eleven years since, something much greater had been lost than pubs and churches, streets and squares. A whole way of life was going under. There were fey touches to the Festival across the river but they had been designed and applied by those outside the charmed circle of what my father had begun to call 'the real Londoners'. These were the very people his own restless ambition had left behind.

But like him, I had started to fabulise the past. The old girl who ran this café leaned on the counter to watch us talk, her hair pinned up haphazardly, her old-fashioned stays shaping a massive chest, protected by a flowered pinny. The air was thick with cigarette smoke and steam, the floor slippery with the rain tramped in by customers . She saw a good-looking man smoking a pipe and a kid dressed in poncey sort of clothes, the sort they all wore nowadays. But the mere fact of our having chosen to come in told her what she wanted to know. We were tribal, just like her.

'How's the chemistry lessons going?' my father asked, breaking his reverie.

'I'm doing better.'

He glanced at me and then shrugged, as though weary of the whole damn mess.

'You should start to think about what you want to do when you leave school,' he said. 'You've had enough school, I should think. Who's this girl your mother's going on about?'

'She *told* you?'

He knocked out his pipe on the tin ashtray in front of us.

'I was going to take you to the Science Museum or something,' he said. 'But I need to get back. You go. Walk down to the Embankment. Any train'll get you there.'

'Mum told you about her?'

'I haven't got time. But if I were you, I'd start thinking about something a bit more important than skirt.'

But it was too late for that. Figgie and I had made our commitments in the changing pavilion of the kiddy paddling pool one moonstruck night. We sat on the low bench, looking out on the little rectangle of star-studded water, beyond which lay a meadow and beyond that a road lined with trees. At our backs was a sandy lane lit by wobbling gas lamps and every so often a cyclist would pass in the dark, tyres hissing. Figgie half lay against the boards of the pavilion, her coat and blouse open, her breasts exposed to my kisses, her hand dangerously in my lap. We were sixteen, the world had lost its place-names and history, time had slowed and stopped.

This sense of how love can erase all that has passed before was one of the most important things that ever happened to me. It was not unique and I have learned since that some people can experience such dense and crowded feelings in other ways, perhaps in nobler causes. Loving Figgie took many twists and turns before it ended but nothing had ever before happened to match that first ecstatic evening. I had found a world that had in it no qualifications or abridgements, no compromises. I held on to her with a passion not to let her get away and – my lips in her hair – not to float away myself.

She was an only child who borrowed from her mother's wardrobe. Her father was a man who drenched his food in gravy. The dog was called Timmy. She too had been to the Festival of Britain and it had been her first visit to London. She could not see what all the fuss was about. She liked the singer Al Martino, worshipped Gregory Peck and would like to have been Rhonda Fleming in another life. Soham Boy had started out fine but really only wanted to get into her knickers. His mother was a toad. School was a lot of laughs and she would be sorry to leave. When she grew older she knew she would be one of those big chunky women that are not fat, but look it. She was very happy to stay in Cambridge all her life. Every dope wanted to go to Paris for a holiday but she would prefer Nice. Or Monte Carlo. For all the running about that I did, I was still painfully thin. My hair must surely be cut with a knife and fork in a darkened room. She liked my shoes. I made her laugh. She loved me.

Chapter Nine

THAT SUMMER, *SOUTH PACIFIC* OPENED IN LONDON
after a two-year run in New York. The star, Mary Martin, was
no stranger to hit shows on Broadway but not so well known
in England, although she had appeared in half a dozen films.
As part of the publicity for her London debut, the *Sunday
Pictorial* ran a 150-word essay competition for which the prizes
were two tickets to the show and – a sophisticated touch – a
cocktail dress for the girl who would help complete a memorable night out. With Figgie in mind, I entered and won.

I think it was one of the few things I ever did in life that
genuinely impressed my mother. When the parcel came, she
was delighted that a mere schoolboy had put one over the
entertainment pages of a national newspaper. This coup had
nothing to do with any talent I might have for stringing a few
words together but was a late and necessary flowering of
cunning and deception. Somewhere in London, some know-
nothing git of a journalist had been tricked into parting with
a not-very-good dress. And wouldn't *his* face be red, Peggy

crowed, to know that it had gone to a kid out in the sticks? It was typical of her to imagine the competition had been run by Londoners for Londoners; after all, who in the Smoke would lift a finger to reward some clodhopping swede?

'Which, after all, you are these days, when you think about it.'

The tickets to *South Pacific* were of much less interest to her. Like me, she had never been to the theatre and supposed they were getting rid of seats from which nothing could be seen, something she had heard was a common design fault of West End theatres. Moreover, the show tunes were already well known on the radio and only a fool would pay money to hear them played live. For her, *four* tickets to the Drury Lane Theatre would have constituted an adequate consolation prize for those who had not conned the *Sunday Pictorial* out of a dress.

The remark about my having become a swede stung. I felt there was a stage waiting for me in London and saw some kind of smoke-filled future hanging round jazz clubs at night and sleeping late in a flat off, say, Charing Cross Road. Immediately after entering the newspaper competition I sent a poem to *John O'London's Weekly*. I got back an amiable handwritten note from the eminent Georgian poet and critic, J. C. Squire, suggesting I read more widely. I can remember the text of the poem: it was about seeing three oranges floating in the lap of the Thames and inferring from them apt comment on something or other – I don't recall what, but something rotten at the heart. It was that kind of bitter pessimism I had to offer the capital, in between the delirium of seeing Figgie naked every day and hanging loose with the jazz crowd at 100 Oxford Street. The new cool was black cotton-knit shirts over imported chinos, ideally topped with a leather fighter-pilot jerkin. I had none of these things yet but the desire was there.

My mother and I opened the parcel together over a cup of tea in the kitchen. The dress came in a grey and mauve cardboard box and was wrapped in silver tissue paper, a detail Peggy found especially impressive. There was even a compliments slip. By a pleasant piece of circularity, the dress had been made up in Great Titchfield Street, down which my father had marched. It was red satin and strapless, the bodice shaped by plastic wire. My mother held it up and examined the label.

'It says here 36. I hope this girl's got something to fill it out. They should have asked you what size you wanted.'

'They did,' I mumbled.

Peggy looked at me with disbelief.

'She must be a big girl,' she said. 'How are you going to smuggle her up to London in this, then?' A second anxious thought hit her. 'And please! Tell me you won't go wearing that horrible bloody suit. You want something dark blue, double-breasted.'

'I thought you might knit me something.'

She pointed her cigarette.

'Now don't get cocky.'

Figgie previewed the dress for me at the Cambridge Jazz Club, where it caused a mild sensation, not least because when jiving, one of her breasts did fall out of the suspect bodice. She shoved it back in without a flicker of shame. There were many things to learn from Figgie and one of them was complete self-possession. She had been raised like a boxer to ride the punch, always to move to the centre of the ring if it were possible. My mother's fears for her were misfounded. She would have gone to London in Josephine Baker's banana skirt and wearing roller skates if the occasion demanded it. My own mortification about the accident was swiftly despatched.

'The dress is crap,' I mourned, walking her home.

'The dress is satin,' she contradicted.

Her mother, whom I had never met, was entranced. She gave me credit for a romantic gesture – it fell out that they took the *Sunday Pictorial* at home and had cut out the winning essay, sticking it to the kitchen wall with a dab of Gloy at each corner. I gave Figgie the theatre tickets to keep safe and her mother, clever woman, rang up Drury Lane to find out where they were on the seating plan. They were centre stalls.

'Let's hope she don't blow you out and go with someone else,' Peggy commented.

'That won't happen.'

But Figgie stealing the tickets was exactly the sort of

betrayal she herself expected from life. Maybe this whole thing was an elaborate plot to humiliate me. I could see her thinking this. Then she smiled, the warmth of it lighting up the kitchen table at which we sat. Impulsively, I reached over and held her hand, the first purely adult gesture I ever made to her. There were tears in her eyes.

'You're jealous,' I joshed her.

'You'll get robbed before you've walked out the station,' she derided, hanging on to my hand with a fierce grip.

'If I don't come home, it means we've both joined the Foreign Legion.'

'Good luck to you,' Peggy said fervently.

We weren't robbed, or not in the station. That came in a small Italian restaurant where we ate before the show. There was far more glamour then in eating out, even at the wrong hour and in a not very distinguished trattoria sandwiched between two shops. We ordered in trepidation, calculating that we would come out with perhaps five shillings in change. Three young waiters came to look down Figgie's front and tease us mercilessly. It was, despite my mother's pleadings, one of the last outings for the zoot suit.

'Gangster!' cried Marco.

At the end of the meal he presented us with two glasses of sambuca and for me a small – a very small – cheroot. We were of course the only diners. As we were leaving, Marco took a carnation from the tin vase on the table and gave it to Figgie. With tremendous aplomb, she gave him her dazzling smile and tapped him on the cheek with the flower. At the door, she relented and let him peck her on the cheek.

'O la bella ragazza!' he cried.

'You are one lucky gangster,' Marco's brother said, removing the cheroot from my fingers. 'Don't smoke in the street. Is not Naples.'

Halfway through *South Pacific*, I realised I was going out with Ensign Nellie Forbush, the part played by Mary Martin. Miss Martin was thirty-eight and only four years younger than my mother: Figgie was sixteen and so radiant that I felt I sat in pools of her reflected light. When it came to pizzazz, to carelesss beauty and – I found the word – style, I was seeing life imitate art. The girl on the stage was the girl in the stalls. We held hands, we laughed, we bit our lips, we cheered. Coming out into the dark of Drury Lane, we walked to the tube at Holborn like initiates coming away from some deep mystery.

'I want to go again tomorrow,' Nellie Forbush said. 'We should go every night for the rest of our lives.'

The last train to Cambridge ran through Waltham Cross, where the houses back on to the line, their gardens drab and defeated in any weather, at any time of the day. It was the last outpost of London, a trolley bus terminus and the northern boundary of the Metropolitan Police. We theatregoers passed this dismal moonlit landscape locked together in an embrace we thought need never end. I did not know it, but less than a year later I would be living in just such a house by the railway line and the red satin dress would be returned to me, cut by pinking shears into coupons the size of postage stamps. Thousands of them.

I can only remember one O-level in any detail. The art examination involved drawing a Hockneyesque still life of a deck chair with a pair of sandals at its base. I had already completed a painting derived from imagination, in which a half-opened packet of sandwiches rested on the stump of a newly felled tree. In the early stages of the painting, which was done in tempera, a small figure was walking towards the viewer, presumably a woodsman on his way to resume his lunch. This might have made the work pleasantly anecdotal but I was dissatisfied with the composition and painted him out. He became a sullen and muddy bush. To add a dash of modernity, the grass was mauve and the sky green. The awful melancholy that resulted has haunted me ever since, all the more so because the candidate next to me had executed an excruciatingly detailed study of a narrow boat passing under a bridge. The sanity and optimism of this painting could have cured the sick and raised the dead.

As for the deck chair, I drew a monstrously enlarged object that might have been an engine for catching falling stars and, for want of space, omitted the sandals. When the work was collected, the art master glanced at me with a half-smile on his lips.

'I think I saw you out with your girl last Saturday,' he murmured. 'Is she any good at this sort of thing?'

I took the remark to mean an unequivocal 'Bye-bye, O-level art'. One down and nine to go. For a week or more we wandered about with scratty bits of paper on which the examination timetable was written, entering the assembly hall like sheep on their way to slaughter. My particular companion was Dillon, a chastened Dillon, because there was a bit of a chance that the delectable Ginny was pregnant.

'Christ!'

'Yeah,' Dillon agreed. 'She's late but it's not certain.'

We had this conversation sitting in the open-sided changing hut at the corner of the practice field. He sat with his head in his hands, his elbows on his knees.

'You should see the house she lives in,' he muttered.

'What are you going to do?'

'Shoot myself. If *I* don't, my father will.'

We smoked in silence for a moment or two and then he looked up and stunned me with the most unexpected, the most electric remark he'd ever made.

'Don't risk it with Figgie.'

'How do you know I haven't?'

'I'm warning you not to.'

He knew it had not come to this because Ginny had told him and she knew because Figgie had told her every twist and turn of our romance. It was my introduction to the politics of love. In succinct form, I was not as free as I thought. We stubbed out our cigarettes and trudged back to sit the maths exam. I said the heartless words every man says to his pal at a time like this.

That night Figgie phoned.

'Tell Pete she's alright,' she said brusquely and rang off before I could utter a word.

When the exam fever was over, a boy called Harris, a rugby player, suggested we go to France together by bike. I was confused by what had happened to Ginny and resented Figgie's sudden coolness. Though I did not know him well, I agreed to go with this boy, the first step of the journey being to acquire a passport. Under the rubric *Occupation* on the title page, I see that I wrote 'Schoolboy', a piece of innocence that now speaks volumes about those Mitchum years.

Figgie was going away for a fortnight and I timed the trip with Teeth Harris to coincide with that. Our plan was to cycle to Dover in a day, cross to Calais and then head for Paris. We were light on clothes but heavy on tinned food because Teeth believed we should do better in camping mode. He was hugely strong and his bike carried the pup tent and a massive frying pan. And we did actually cycle all the way to Dover in a day, a very long and vexing day in which the bikes had to be walked up even the slightest gradient. It was eleven at night when we reached the port and we bought fish and chips before retracing our steps a little and sleeping in a park. We fell on to the morning ferry and lay down on deck, depressed and exhausted.

But in Calais our spirits revived. We found a café and asked for wine. We were refused. There happened to be four Swedish sailors in from a timber boat moored a little way down the quay and they adopted us. We swapped cigarettes for beer with these pirates and pretended not to notice they were already Scandinavian drunk. The session lasted from eleven in the morning until five in the afternoon, at which time we found our bikes and wobbled our way out of town, coming to rest in a field of potatoes. We stopped only once, to buy two small bottles of peach brandy which we supposed to be the drink of Parisian sophisticates.

'No need to put the tent up,' Teeth decided.

We dragged it over us and let the rain pelt down. The peach brandy we had glugged was the most vile concoction I had ever tasted and seemed to coat my teeth with cobwebs.

'This is the life,' Teeth said. Mud from the potato rows was caught in his hair and a drenched and unlit cigarette clung to his lips. 'The real experience,' he added, in a distant voice.

'Do we need to eat tonight?' I asked tentatively.

'Eat later,' he said, his eyelids flickering.

'Maybe we should have bought some bread and cheese.'

'There's three tins of baked beans in that saddlebag,' he pointed out. 'And stewed steak. And peas. Live like princes. But tomorrow.'

It was hardly past six o'clock. The farmer found us at seven. He moved us out of his field and on to a patch of grass. We spent an hour putting up the tent, chuckling like maniacs. Then we crawled inside and slept the clock round.

We never got to Paris, defeated by cobbled roads and cheap alcohol. The lowest point of the trip came when we wandered through a stand of pines by the coast and found a sandy hollow to our liking. It was night and we pitched the tent at least to the extent of inserting the poles and spreading out the stained cotton. In the morning we were woken by three polite Frenchmen who pointed out that we were in a fairway bunker of the very prestigious Le Touquet golf course. One of the player's balls was trapped under our bikes. With extraordinary tact and good humour we were ushered out the way we had come in.

'Embarrassing,' Teeth said. 'I say we find a quiet beach, wash the clothes and generally spruce ourselves up.'

We did. The great hit of that summer was Kaye Starr's 'The Wheel of Fortune', a song we howled three or four times a day. We sat in the dunes stark naked, drinking red wine, watching our clothes dry and singing. Teeth proffered a bottle of olive oil, which he used for sun block. His own chest and belly glistened.

'The French are okay,' he said. 'Except there are no girls around.'

He eyed me speculatively.

'You're going out with that Figgie, eh? How long do you think that'll last?'

'You don't think it will?'

'Say when you're in the sixth and she's at work?'

'I shan't be going into the sixth.'

'You got ten O-levels, didn't you?'

This was true. When the first notification came from school, I had stared at it with incredulity. I knew dozens of gifted boys in my year and the thought of having joined them was as big a surprise as would have been winning the football pools or getting a cable from 20th Century Fox. There was no particular grandeur about it and delighting in the results was for the most part a solitary pleasure, for my parents had no true way of measuring academic success. My father's eye passed swiftly down the list.

'I see I passed chemistry then,' he quipped.

Teeth had scraped five but failed English Language, a thing he intended to put right in a resit. He had actually asked me the secret of writing a passable essay while cranking along in the merciless summer heat.

'Are *you* going to stay on?' I asked.

'I'm going to be somebody,' he said, very calm.

While he dozed, I studied him. He was one of those lucky people who go brown in the slightest sun. After nine days of drunken squabbling he had at last said something interesting. Here was this boy shaped like a man, almost, about whom I knew very little. We were not in the same class and shared no lessons. Though we had spent the same amount of time learning French, his own was practically non-existent. On that first day with the Swedish sailors he had staggered up from the table saying, 'I'm just going to go to the Pernod.' I should have been forewarned. There was at the time a little oval plaque advertising the aperitif and his eye had been caught by one screwed to a door beside the bar. He pushed it open with a flourish and stumbled into a room where the patron sat eating mussels and talking to his more intimate friends.

It was I who had gone into shops for wine and peaches, I who had negotiated with the fearsome motor-cycle *douanes* on the road to Montreuil and apologised to the golfers playing a championship course at Paris-by-the-Sea. About France, I was as confused as he was, noticing not only the absence of girls but the eerie emptiness of the villages we passed through. The Pas-de-Calais was by no means as enticing as Paris, which I would not visit for another five years. Yet none of these things was of greater importance than the one big thing – that this amiable but slow companion with the beautifully sculpted body could contemplate going to university. When the Wrestler said he was going where the levers of power were to be found, it made sense. For him to be joined there by Teeth, with his penchant for nudity and his unchallenged mind, was a thoroughly disconcerting idea.

I knew my own future, for it had been decided for me by my father. As soon as the examination fortnight was over, he told me I had read enough books for a lifetime and should learn about the real world. He ordered me to seek a temporary job with the Post Office while I found my bearings. He even specified the job. When I got back from staring with envy at the naked Teeth, with his tapering thighs and rippling stomach, I was to start as a telegram messenger boy.

The arrangements of the Telegram Office could hardly have been any simpler. The messengers sat on greasy wooden benches in an unlit room and shuffled on their backsides towards a hatch in the wall, through which the pale orange envelopes would be thrust. Without the door being left open, the space would have been totally dark. The walls were decorated with names, the names of football players, and highly imaginative drawings of girls – and in one of two places huge penises firing what looked like tracer bullets. Unconsciously, the telegram boys had responded to this office as the prison it was.

Outside, the red bikes were ranged in stands. You received the telegram, glanced at the address, put it into a pouch that was attached to a leather belt, squared off the pillbox hat and cycled away. My very first delivery was to a terrace of early Victorian houses opposite Addenbrooke's Hospital. Mr Spence, the recipient, tore the envelope open on his doorstep.

'Ah,' he said with keenly managed emotion. 'I have just been awarded the architectural contract for the new Coventry Cathedral. Splendid.'

He pulled out a handful of change and after studying it on the palm of his hand for a few moments, selected a sixpence.

'Thank you so much,' he murmured, and then added, glancing into the street, 'Is it raining?'

I went back to the office, sat down on the bench at the point nearest to the door and waited twenty minutes for a delivery to a street off Mill Road. The woman who received it sank slowly to her knees and laid her head on the frayed carpet. After a moment or two, she looked up at me with tears streaming down her face. She held out a bony hand for me to pull her up.

'No reply,' she said, broken.

My father was, by his own lights, teaching me a lesson. I think he was also paying me back for what he perceived as treachery in the war years. The other telegram boys soon had my number. For a grammar school berk to have joined the office was a clear indication of something having gone very wrong. On the third day at work I had the second and final fist fight of my life. A hugely fat boy laid me out on the floor with the first clear punch of the scuffle. There was sniggering as I groped about for a way to stand up. Tortoise, the clerk who handed out the telegrams, stuck his head out of the hatch. He looked about as happy to work for the Post Office as a sweeper in a morgue, a beaten grey-faced man with a wen under one eye.

'I hope you ain't going to cause trouble,' he said.

The obvious question about all this was put by Figgie (five O-levels, credit in biology).

'Do you have to do everything your dad tells you to do?'

'No,' I said doubtfully.

'He sounds a bit barmy.'

'My mother's the barmy one.'

'No, it's not her.' Figgie said. 'It's him.'

We walked out to the west of Cambridge along field paths and sat in copses that we made our own from frequent visits. I was terribly aware of her body but too scared to lose her by touching her. The business with Ginny had come between us – and now there was this farcical and demeaning job, pushing a red bike round Cambridge, delivering what was almost always bad news in the parts of the city we knew best, and only good news to the parts we would probably never get to know at all. The head porter at King's expressed it well. Tapping the edge of the telegram envelope on his desk, he puffed his pipe and gave me a friendly smile.

'Affairs of state, eh? It must be a bleeding honour for you to do your job. How I wish I was young.'

It all made no sense at all to Figgie.

'I love you,' I said on one of these gloomy excursions into the countryside.

'I know you do. But where does that get you?'

'With you I can be somebody,' I said, adapting Teeth's remark made in the dunes. She held my hand, tears forming in her eyes.

'I never wanted to go to university or anything like that. I want to work somewhere interesting and be happy and be *ordinary*. Go to the flicks, just be like everyone else. I don't understand what's made you as complicated as you are. You make me laugh, we like the same things, mostly. But I just don't understand what it is inside you.'

'Nothing,' I suggested.

'That's rubbish. It frightens me when you talk like that.'

We made love a week later, not out in the woods but at home, on top of my bed. My mother was out with Neil and we undressed and lay down on the brown kapok cover my father had bought from the GI surplus store in Mill Road. However Figgie thought I lived, nothing could have prepared her for that back bedroom and its seedy arrangements. We could not pull the curtains because there were none. There was a bedside lamp but two pieces of flex had been joined together by Elastoplast and I was terrified that either she or I would step on the junction and drop dead of electrocution even before we had undressed. What books I had were piled up on the floor and, leaning against them, the dozen or so records I had bought. The battered wind-up gramophone on which they were played seemed to me especially shaming. There was a carpet but it felt damp to the touch of my naked feet, something I had never before noticed. It was altogether a horrible place to be.

'I've never done this before,' Figgie whispered as we hugged, fear making our skins wet with sweat.

'Then don't let's do it now.'

She pushed me away and lay on her back. She raised her knees.

'Don't ever tell anyone,' she said. A silver bracelet slipped from her wrist to her forearm. There was a strand of hair caught in the corner of her mouth. She closed her eyes.

If I do betray her, it is because that afternoon, so rushed and incoherent and at the same time so mysteriously timeless, has stuck in my mind as the pattern experience of growing up. From Figgie I learned all that I could ever have hoped about love, and trust, and generosity. When today I see boys embracing girls at late-night bus stops or as figures in a landscape past which the train hurtles, it makes my heart lurch. They may look foolish, they may lack sense altogether, but there is a sweetness about them that flies like an arrow. Being sixteen is a tribulation as much as an ecstasy and nobody can find happiness alone.

There is one more deal of the cards before this story ends. I was cycling back from a telegram delivery one afternoon when the headmaster stepped out into the crowded roadway and stopped me by the simple expedient of seizing the tail of my jacket.

'What is this?' he asked.

'Um –'

'Do you have any idea how many people in the entire *county* managed ten O-levels? The answer is three. *Three.* Of whom you are one. I would like to know what the hell you think you are doing riding about in that silly hat.'

'My father wants me to –'

'Yes, I should very much like to meet your father. In fact, you can tell him that I will be round to see him this evening.'

'He only comes home at weekends.'

'Then I shall see him on Saturday. Tell him that. At six in the evening.'

'He won't see you.'

'Oh yes, he will,' the headmaster promised. He looked at me more closely. 'You are the horrible little squit that I had to beat once for making a fool of yourself in a biology lesson, aren't you?'

'Yessir.'

'I thought so. What did you think when you passed in ten subjects? Were you for example slightly elated? Did you toast yourself in Tizer?'

'I supposed a lot of people had done the same.'

'Time to wake up, then. We can do something with you. Six o'clock Saturday.'

My father took a dim view of this visit. When the headmaster knocked at the door on the dot of six, he walked with deliberate slowness to answer. He stood in the doorway, smoking a manly Capstan.

'Yes?'

'This is my daughter Olivia,' the Head indicated. 'May we come in for a moment?'

'I don't think we have a lot to discuss,' AJT said.

'I think we do. I believe you were in the RAF? What rank had you?'

'I was a flight lieutenant, chum.'

'I left as a wing commander. And I'm not specially your chum. Now be a good chap and let me in.'

The two-year-old Olivia was passed to me and we walked hand in hand to the kitchen, where my mother was hiding behind the door with Neil. AJT and the Head went into the front room. He, not my father, closed the door.

'Now there'll be fireworks,' Peggy said. 'Well, they won't be able to pin anything on me. I shall deny everything. And if you keep your yap shut we'll get out of it. Whatever it is.'

We gave Olivia a glass of American soda, with a glacé cherry riding on its surface. After a few minutes, Bryn Newton John came to collect his daughter and was ushered out by my father with far more ceremony than that which he had entered. The two men shook hands on the doorstep. AJT closed the door and turned to me, fumbling for another cigarette.

'Monday morning, you give your notice,' he said. 'You go into the sixth form when the new term starts. And you work. No more pissing around, you understand? Now wipe that look off your face and get out there and mow the lawn.'

'What the bloody hell's the sixth form?' my mother demanded, taking the cherry from its glass and passing it for my brother to chew. AJT turned on his heel and retreated to the front room. The noise he made with the scuffed and dusty door rang like a rifle shot. Peggy turned to me.

'Well?' she asked.